TRAIL OF THE SNAKE

TRAIL
OF THE
SNAKE
FROM BIG BEND TO BAJA

by

MICHAEL A. WILLIAMSON

SUNSTONE PRESS

SANTA FE

Sunstone books may be purchased for educational, business, or sales promotional use. For information please write: Special Markets Department, Sunstone Press, P.O. Box 2321, Santa Fe, New Mexico 87504-2321.

Book and Cover design ▸ Vicki Ahl
Body typeface ▸ Bell MT
Printed on acid free paper

Library of Congress Cataloging-in-Publication Data

Williamson, Michael A., 1942-.
  Trail of the snake : from Big Bend to Baja / by Michael A. Williamson.
      p. cm.
  Includes index.
  ISBN 978-0-86534-752-6 (softcover : alk. paper)
  1. Williamson, Michael A., 1942- 2. Snakes—Collection and preservation.
  3. Reptiles—Collection and preservation. 4. Herpetologists—United States—Biography.
  5. Biologists—United States—Biography. I. Title.
  QL31.W567A3 2010
  597.96092—dc22
                                    2010002160

Published in

WWW.SUNSTONEPRESS.COM
SUNSTONE PRESS / POST OFFICE BOX 2321 / SANTA FE, NM 87504-2321 /USA
(505) 988-4418 / ORDERS ONLY (800) 243-5644 / FAX (505) 988-1025

"We have met the enemy and he is us.
—Walt Kelly

CONTENTS

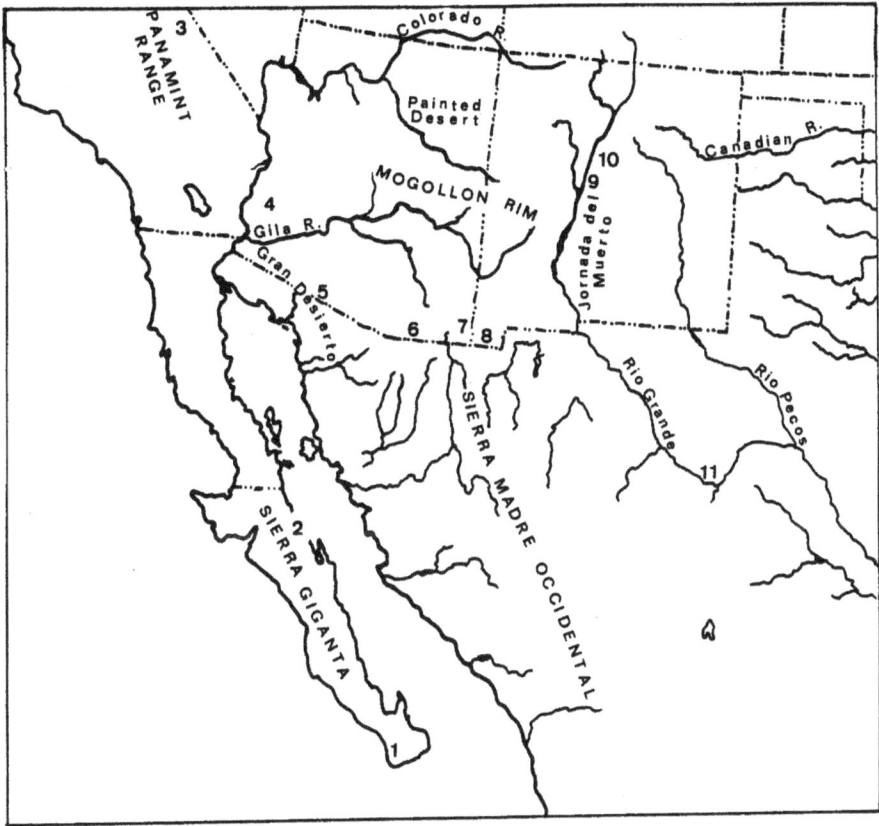

POINTS OF INTEREST MENTIONED IN THE TEXT

(1) La Burrera
(2) Poacher's Camp
(3) Bad Water
(4) Palm Canyon
(5) Organ Pipe
(6) Hamburg Mine
(7) Onion Saddle
(8) Animas Peak
(9) The "Dunes"
(10) Black-tail Den
(11) Terlingua Creek

FOREWORD

This book is the result of more than 50 years of accumulated field and research experience. It is undertaken at the urging of friends and acquaintances who have patiently and graciously listened to my many stories of intrepid travelers who, having braved searing desert heat, blinding sandstorms and all manner of fearsome and fascinating creatures in their relentless pursuit of knowledge, have experienced a sense of joy and wonderment which can only be felt by communing with nature.

Of course I can not assume all of the credit. I would like to thank my parents, whose patience and support during my formative years allowed me to pursue my somewhat "unusual" pastime; or at least they thought so at the time. I am profoundly grateful for the spirit of cooperation shown by my wife Mabel, and two daughters, all of whom have adjusted admirably to living in a house filled with snakes and other sorts of crawling things; at one time as many as 140 including alligators, Gila monsters, cobras and a fourteen foot reticulated python named Luther. Mabel also reads my manuscripts and offers helpful suggestions. I also want to extend my gratitude to Jessie Applegarth who typed the finished manuscript for original edition of this book. Finally my special thanks goes to Bill Degenhardt, without whose encouragement and advice this book might never have been written.

And to R. DeWitt Ivey, my former high school biology teacher, whose standards for excellence are tempered only by his compassion and understanding for his students.

I would like to add that it was in pursuit of my career as a herpetologist that I became exposed to the happy hobby of photography, an indispensable tool of any naturalist. No creature, great or small, is ever safe from the probing eye of my camera lens. Of course, traveling about the country photographing animals as I have done can become expensive and so I have, from time to time, found it necessary to seek gainful employment in order that I might support my habit. These experiences, although they have frequently been meaningful and enriching, are as often as not a source of distraction from more serious academic endeavors. Such diversions include, among others, the teaching of high school science, freelance writing, a short stint as a curatorial assistant at the Museum of Southwestern Biology (UNM) and the somewhat dubious distinction of having been appointed the first curator of birds and reptiles at the Rio Grande Zoological Park; a position which I held for five years and one week.

And now I hope you will sit back in your favorite chair and embark upon a journey with me, a journey that will take us from the Pecos to the Colorado, and beyond; from the depths of Death Valley to the towering peaks of the Sierra Madre Occidental; from Big Bend to Baja. We will visit places with names like Onion Saddle, Ajo Road and the Hamburg Mine. And we will meet many interesting people along the way, some of whom are life-long friends.

This is my story of travel and adventure; whether it be witnessing the incredible bravery of a mother hawk defending her nest in a fight to the finish against a hungry great-horned owl, an encounter with an enraged female black bear defending her cubs against the indiscretions of a human intruder or, perhaps, listening to the melodious call of a red-winged blackbird defiantly proclaiming its territorial legacy. We will encounter many marvelous creatures along the way; a snake that "walks" across the hot desert sands, another so deadly that its venom is reported to kill a human in twenty minutes; a lizard that "barks" like a dog and another that actually runs a fever when it is ill. And, last, a species of lizard in which there are no males, only females. All these creatures and many more will be met in the following pages, and hopefully they will become your friends as they have become mine. For all living things—even the poisonous ones—are a part of the overall scheme of things; the intricate inter-relationship of all life. Surely man's own salvation lies in his ability to learn to live in harmony with the living things around him.

EARLY DAYS

As a youngster, I was privileged to spend many happy hours fishing with my grandfather. It was during these memorable excursions that I became acquainted with the many wild creatures that abound along the margins of lakes and streams. Thus it was not at all unnatural that I should have become fascinated by this creature or that from time to time. Nor, I suppose, that I should have brought a few of them home with me.

Turtles held a special fascination for me and I somehow managed to convince my cousin—who convinced my aunt—that what they really needed was a water-filled moat in the back yard. This done, we proceeded to stock it with a motley assortment of appealing creatures: pond sliders, soft-shelled turtles, bullfrogs, catfish, carp, mosquito fish, crawdads, and just about anything else that we chanced across.

Things were going well until one day I tactfully suggested to my aunt that her basement would make an ideal place for breeding crocodiles. "It has a uniform temperature," I explained, "a southern exposure, water, a drain...it's perfect..." The anticipated enthusiasm failed to materialize in my aunt's expressionless gaze.

So, in the spring of 1957, the turtle pond was quickly drained and filled in. A devastating blow! Despite repeated attempts to convince my aunt, however, she remained adamant; to encourage such minor vices as turtle ponds could only lead to more serious transgressions. I strongly suspected, though, that she just didn't *like* crocodiles.

Early one morning in the summer of 1958 I was fishing in a stream above Fenton Lake, situated in the Jemez Mountains of north-central New Mexico. The fishing had been good all morning and I had a full string of rainbow trout, a species not native to the state.

As the daytime temperatures rose, the fish slackened their feeding and I decided that this would be a good time to do some cleaning. I tossed the "innards" of each cleaned fish back into the stream, as I was accustomed to doing. After a while I noticed a completely submerged snake engulfing the discarded entrails.

Fascinated, I watched for some time before reaching down and gently lifting him from the water. The garter snake squirmed around, disgorging some of its meal. When this failed to elicit its freedom, it resorted to the garter snake's most formidable weapon; emitting large quantities of musk from specialized glands (with which all garter snakes are endowed) it proceeded to smear this foul and odious substance liberally over my wrist and forearm.

By the following day I had acquired three more garter snakes and two bull snakes. I had just been initiated into the happy hobby of snake collecting...although I had little idea at the time the extent to which this seemingly insignificant event had altered the course of my life: I've been looking for snakes ever since.

In late October of that same year, I was hiking along a ridge overlooking Tijeras Canyon, about fifteen miles east of Albuquerque. The night had been cool, but now the rock face captured the warming rays of the morning sun. In the solitude of the mountain nothing moved; even the breeze was calm. A fence lizard, startled by my presence, bobbed anxiously before vanishing into an abandoned pack rat's nest.

Suddenly my attention was drawn to a splash of yellow and brown against the gray limestone. It was the velvet coils of a black-tailed rattlesnake. As the symmetrical loops followed one another into the safety of a nearby crevice, I marveled at the grace and beauty of this much-maligned creature which had so silently withdrawn from my gaze. As my eyes adjusted to the darkness of its retreat, I could see the flickering tongue searching nervously for some hint as to the intentions of this intruder in its domain.

As I stood gazing down into the canyon below, miniature automobiles made their way back and forth along the distant ribbon of highway. The world seemed very far away. I suddenly became aware of an intense feeling of loneliness; perhaps a premonition.

I turned and began making my way down the slope. On my right was a large opening in the rocks. This was the "den" where large numbers of rattlesnakes had, for untold millennia, spent their winters in that state of dormancy we call hibernation.

The discovery of this lone black-tail represented a range extension for the species, as it had not been previously known to occur in the Sandia Mountains. Consequently, it should have been no surprise that when I informed a high school classmate, Ted Brown, about my discovery, it was at first greeted with a certain amount of skepticism. As I described the snake—the dark mask between the eyes and the black tail—his skepticism soon turned to enthusiasm. We were both excited as we made plans to return to the area the following weekend. We could only hope that an unexpected cold spell would not send the snakes into hibernation for the winter.

Our fears did not materialize; that first weekend in November was unseasonably warm. We left shortly after sunrise, armed with canteens, hooks, pillowcases and lunch. A tree lizard watched as we unloaded our gear from the jeep, his intricate pattern blending almost perfectly with the lichen-encrusted boulders.

We set out at a steady pace up the steep slope leading to the den, neither of us pausing to catch his breath. Making our way between patches of prickly pear and cholla cactus, undaunted by loose rocks shifting beneath our feet, we climbed nearer and nearer to the top. As we approached the den, Ted suddenly stopped, motionless.

"There they are!" he said in a suppressed tone. My own heart jumped as I turned to look at the spot where his hook was pointing. Three black-tails, all adults, were coiled on a ledge just in front of the den. A truly magnificent sight!

Ted made a swift move toward the snakes and deftly hooked the two smaller ones into the open. The third—and largest—was rapidly making its way towards an opening in the rocks. My hook blocked its path. The snake, thus thwarted in its attempt to escape, instinctively threw itself into a defensive coil. I turned to see how Ted was faring. He had already "pinned" his first snake and was preparing to bag it. I held the bag (or in this instance, the pillowcase) open wide, while Ted lowered the writhing serpent into it. The second was pinned and bagged as expeditiously as the first. Now it was my turn... I cautiously maneuvered my snake out of the rocks and onto open ground with my hook.

My knees wobbled slightly as I pinned the head of number three (who was all the while rattling furiously). Holding the hook with my left hand, I firmly grasped the snake's head with my right. Gripping the snake's jaws between my thumb and middle finger, I placed my index finger squarely between its eyes. Releasing the hook, I picked up the snake and lowered it into the waiting pillowcase.

With the third snake securely bagged, we began retracing our steps back down the mountain. We were both too excited about the success of our venture to talk. We were approaching a dense stand of Apache plume when, out of the corner of my eye, I noticed a large striped whipsnake, head and neck raised in typical whipsnake fashion, watching us from behind a small boulder. I was about to point out its position to Ted when it slowly lowered its head and then swiftly disappeared among the rocks.

We returned to the jeep and, with the pillowcases and their contents placed carefully between Ted's feet, headed back into the afternoon sun. Although we didn't know it at the time, this was to be the first of many such pleasant excursions that Ted and I would make together, molding a friendship that was to last for more than half a century.

From those of us who have learned the hard way, "word travels fast." As it happened, the den we had visited that day soon achieved some notoriety amongst local collectors. Whereas it was possible to see as many as fifty rattlesnakes in one day at this den in the late 1950's and early 1960's, this did not remain the case for long. A decade of ravages by overzealous collectors, showing crass disregard for habitat, coupled with the record cold winter of 1971 (when the temperature at the Tijeras Ranger Station dropped to thirty degrees below zero) had apparently annihilated this population. Year after year I returned the den only to find that the snakes had not returned.

Then, in the spring of 1981, I made one more trip to the den. Even though I had no expectation of seeing any snakes, I wanted to take a few photographs for nostalgia. To my surprise, the loop of a snake coil was barely visible under a large rock. A pair of black-tails! I removed the snakes for photographs and then replaced them beneath the rock. It was a sentimental moment.

One chilly day in late February, Ted Brown and I were down at Tingley Beach, which parallels the river in the Bosque part of Albuquerque. We were looking for turtles which might have been brought out of hibernation by a recent warming trend and associated rise in barometric pressure.

The ground was wet between patches of melting snow. Here and there, clumps of grass and leaf debris afforded a dry spot. Although the sun was shining, the snow tenaciously refused to melt.

It was on one such clump of high ground that I discovered, much to my surprise, a mating trio of common garter snakes. The female was the largest, fully twice as large in girth as either of the two males. Both males were attempting to breed simultaneously, apparently with some success. "What have we here?" I thought as I reached down and took hold of the writhing mass of snakes.

I got a good grip on one of the males; number two male, however, managed to struggle free—no mean achievement considering the nature of the sexes, especially their anatomical structure. Each of a snake's two hemipenes may be independently everted during copulation, and must be re-inverted, due to the nature of certain spinous embellishments, to allow removal without injury to either participant.

The female took immediate offense, spreading her jaws and striking vigorously—a response which I felt was out of proportion to the situation (putting myself in her "shoes," perhaps not totally unwarranted, however). There was no need to take hold of the female; she had hold of me! For my part, this was the first time I had observed snakes mating, and I was understandably intrigued by the entire operation. I easily bagged the first male, but the second male had already made good his exit and was who knows where.

When Ted and I measured the female, we found her to be 50" total length—a near record.

The following September found me taking in the sights and sounds of the New Mexico State Fair. It was a hot and dusty day. People were crowded onto the midway, and food concessionaires were busily chasing flies away from the cotton candy and caramel apples.

Making my way through the crowds, I found myself in front of a large trailer covered with murals depicting jungle scenes with all manner of fearsome and ferocious beasts lurking amongst the dense, green foliage. In one scene a young lady, scantily clad in the tattered remnants of a jaguar pelt, was wrapped in the coils of a giant serpent. The serpent gazed with expectation upon his helpless and struggling prey.

Against the din of jungle drums, the loudspeaker blared, "Step right up folks—don't be afraid—its perfectly safe." The barker sat atop a high stool behind a podium in front of the trailer. In one hand he held a microphone, and in the other a roll of tickets which he dispensed to his audience at 25 cents per.

Quite a large crowd had gathered, and they were all standing on their tiptoes to see the five foot boa constrictor he had entwined around his neck. "He's just a baby, folks," he was saying, "but you can see his mother on the inside. See the deadly mamba of Africa, giant constrictors from the Orient—you'll see them all." He looked down at me and smiled as I handed him my quarter. "Step right this way!"

I was amazed by what I saw. Never before had I seen such an assortment of snakes; not the usual lackluster, emaciated types—these snakes were exceedingly well kept and well cared for animals. As I entered, a puff adder almost three feet long—and as big as my calf—puffed menacingly, cocking its head and emitting a loud hiss. Simultaneously its body swelled to almost unbelievable proportions, as if any additional convincing was at all necessary. I stood very still, taking care not to make the snake strike the glass and thereby injure itself.

There were other exotic snakes: cobras, anacondas...and one reticulated python that must have been well over 20 feet. I spent several hours standing there, absorbed in everything I saw.

When I came out the crowd had thinned. The man on the stool was replacing his boa into its sack. He was a heavy set man, with thinning hair combed straight back. His face and hands were deeply tanned from continuous exposure to the sun. "Come over here for a minute." he said, motioning with his hand. "Do you like snakes?" I nodded, adding that I had a small collection at home—mostly rattlesnakes.

As we talked I could see that he had a genuine enthusiasm for his work and a sincere concern for his charges. He told me that his name was Gordon and that he wintered in Florida, making the circuit during the summer months.

He was also interested in photography and was especially interested in photographing a black-tailed rattlesnake, asking if I might know where he could acquire one. I had an unusually pretty juvenile at the time and offered to bring it back with me the following day. He seemed pleased at this.

Then he showed me a book containing excellent color pictures of reptiles and amphibians, which he agreed to let me take home if I would promise to bring it back before the end of the Fair. He also showed me where he had a ladder set up to get over the wall, rather than having to walk all the way around to the gate each time he went in or out. He said it was all right for me to use it since I was, after all, doing business with the carnival.

When I arrived the next day, Mr. Gordon was very busy. He glanced at the pillowcase I was carrying, reached into his pocket, and took out a twenty-dollar bill. "Would you take this over to the midway office and get me another roll of tickets?" he asked. I returned a few minutes later and handed him the roll of tickets. He never broke his patter as he opened the roll and began dispensing tickets to his customers.

As the crowd dwindled he turned to me with a smile, "Well, what have you got in the sack?" I handed him the pillowcase. As he untied the knot, he motioned to his assistant, a tall, thin, almost emaciated-looking fellow who had an obvious liking for his boss, and introduced this young man as "Cross-country."

"That's a real beauty!" Mr. Gordon exclaimed. "What would you take for him?"

"A viper," I said unhesitatingly. At the same time, I cautiously removed the rattlesnake from the pillowcase, holding it with the same three-finger grip I described earlier. Mr. Gordon directed "Cross-country" to put the young black-tail into one of the empty cages, and let me pick out one of the Russel's vipers (or "tic-polonga," as it is called in India) which he kept under his bunk in the rear of the trailer.

"Cross-country" reached out and took the rattlesnake from my hand, holding the snake's jaws closed between his thumb and forefinger in an improvised grip which I have never seen before nor since.

Dropping the snake into a gunny sack, off he went, disappearing around the corner of the trailer. I followed. The small room where the two men slept was partitioned off at one end of the trailer. As my eyes slowly became accustomed to the darkness of the room, I could see that bunk beds had been constructed along one side, and a large trunk was set against the wall opposite the door. A stack of books gathered dust in one corner at the head of the bunk. Among these musty tomes I recognized some old friends: Wright and Wright's *Handbook of Snakes*, Raymond Ditmars' *Reptiles of North America* and, of course, K. P. Schmidt's *Field Book of Snakes*. Some of the others were too tattered to recognize. In the opposite corner stood a stack of wooden frame cages covered with wire. In the top cage I could make out the coils of several snakes, all intertwined. At least half a dozen heads protruded from the top of the coils. I recognized them as the Indian or "spectacled" cobra (so called because of the curious design resembling a pair of eyeglasses which is visible when the snakes spread their hoods).

"Cross-country" now lifted the cage containing the cobras in order to get at one of the empty cages underneath—or so he thought, for the bottom of the cage had not been securely fastened to the sides. Starting across the room with the empty cage top, it suddenly dawned on "C.C." that something was amiss. With a casual shrug, he turned and looked back at the cobras, which by now had realized their opportunity and were struggling to untangle themselves in order to make good their escape. "I'll have to fix that one of these days," was his unconcerned response. He replaced the top of the cage and, lifting it by the bottom this time, placed it on one of the bunks.

He now put his foot on the neck of the gunnysack and untied the knot he had previously fashioned. He then placed the bag, snake and all, in one of the cages.

He then reached under the bunks and retrieved what looked like a weathered old suitcase, placing it on the floor between our feet. I was still standing in the doorway, my hands on the door jamb, my heels hanging over the sill. There were no outside steps, and the floor of the trailer was about four feet above grade.

As "Cross-country" opened the suitcase, I saw three fine-looking Russell's vipers, somewhat dazed by the sudden glare of daylight. Using the same grip he had applied to the rattlesnake, "C.C." reached down with a sudden motion and came up with one of the deadly snakes. He had the expression of a proud father. "I like this one," he said. "It's the best eater, too." He held it out for my inspection.

"It's very nice," I replied, holding out my open pillowcase. These snakes are reported to kill thousands of people every year and, by some accounts, are even more feared than the dreaded cobra.

"I've got something else you'd like to see," he said. Then, without waiting for a response, he reached under the bunk again and pulled out a large footlocker. As he lifted the lid, my heart stopped. He was staring directly up into the eyes of a fourteen-foot king cobra, hood spread!

I shifted my weight backwards and dropped to the ground,

casually walking away as if nothing had happened. I never saw "Cross-country" again.

I returned the book on time. I also traded a young prairie kingsnake for a rosy boa that Mr. Gordon was offering for five dollars. Then he told me to look under the trailer for a wooden box containing an assortment of rattlesnakes; I was to select one for myself. I found the box and opened it. There before me were a red diamond rattlesnake, several sidewinders of assorted sizes and colors, and a pair of tiger rattlesnakes. I selected a young sidewinder, one with a definite pinkish cast to it.

A sad addendum to this story is worth repeating here , as it may save others from having the same experience. Having placed the sidewinder in what I hoped were comfortable surroundings, I introduced a small mouse. This mouse was a runt, much smaller than its litter mates. Even so, when I returned to the room several hours later, I found that the mouse had killed the sidewinder and had eaten both its rattle and its lower jaw! It may seem incredible, but the following day this same mouse managed to kill a five-foot diamondback rattlesnake. I learned my lesson the hard way; never leave a live rodent alone with a snake.

I have spent many enjoyable days hiking in the foothills east of Albuquerque, New Mexico with Lee Anderson during what I can only refer to as our "formative" years—when the excitement was in the hunt and acquisition was only a secondary consequence. Our favorite collecting spot was in Juan Tabo Canyon, at the north end of the Sandia Mountains.

One morning late in May of 1960, Lee and I were hiking up the arroyo that formed the main branch of the canyon. The sun was barely peeking over the crest of the mountain, and long shadows played tricks on our eyes. We breathed deeply as we walked, taking in the crisp fresh mountain air. Although the air was cool there was no wind, which was unusual for this time of year; it promised to be a beautiful day.

We had been walking for about twenty minutes when, almost simultaneously, we both stopped, our eyes transfixed on a low overhang of granite, beneath which was coiled a large diamondback! The diamondback's head rested comfortably in the center of its coils, and the only indication that it was even aware of our presence was the slow, deliberate probing of its forked tongue.

Now meeting a large diamondback face to face for the first time on its own turf sends a chill up and down the spine. Neither Lee nor I had ever collected a snake of this magnitude before. I figured it to be four or five feet long, but very stout—with a large head—and at the time it appeared much larger than it really was. Lee generously proclaimed that I could have it and promptly sat down on a convenient rock to watch and see what I would do next.

I hooked the snake out into the open where it immediately assumed the raised, s-shaped, loop which is a species trademark. After several tense moments I managed to "pin" its head in the loose gravel of the arroyo bottom. As I took a firm grip on the head, the snake began to thrash about violently. It was all I could do to hang on with both hands! Lee could no longer sit idly by.

He jumped off the rock and held open the pillowcase for me. Our coordinated movements were like precision clockwork. We worked reflexively, there being no time for deliberations. The snake already had his strategy figured out, and when he saw the sack he seemed to explode in a fury which I would not have thought imaginable. I through the snake into the sack and, in the same motion, reached for the hook. I held the hook out horizontally as Lee folded the neck of the sack over it, thereby preventing the snake from shooting back out again. We now laid the sack, snake and all, on the ground and, placing the handle of the hook across the opening, tied the bag securely.

Then we both sat down to rest our nerves and organize our thoughts; it had all happened so fast. One thing we knew for sure, though; we had bagged one heck of a rattler. I looked down at my T-shirt; it was splattered with venom. There was also venom on the handle of the snake hook where the snake had managed one good bite before I was able to get its head pinned.

I don't think either one of us would have wanted to try pinning that snake on hard ground, for in its wild thrashing it could very easily have fractured its neck vertebrae.

On another occasion Lee and I were in Juan Tabo in search of lizards for snake food. This was early in the spring when it was still too chilly at night for most snakes to be out moving around. I was carrying only stout rubber bands, which I use to stun lizards that are too wary to be approached by hand, and a small tobacco sack in which to transport the captives.

Lee had gone up one of the side canyons, and I another. The climb was becoming steeper, and in places I found it necessary to assist with my hands. The sun was shining directly onto the south-facing slope, a circumstance which had evidently lured a small black-tail which was now sunning itself—or so I supposed—in an open area below a rocky outcrop.

The snake made no move at my approach, not even the usual telltale tongue-flick. Curiosity began to get the better of me. Could it be dead? I approached cautiously, moving slowly on my hands and knees. The opacity of its eyes was a clear indication that this snake was about to go into a shed. But now I noticed something else: the pupils were rolled forward to the "corner" of the eyes. This snake was sound asleep, completely oblivious to my presence!

Slowly I reached down and gently lifted the snake, holding its head and body as one might handle a delicate piece of china ware. The snake offered no resistance nor did it offer to bite, or even attempt to rattle. It has been my experience over the years that this sort of placid behavior on the part of black-tails is the rule rather than the exception—at least for New Mexico black-tails.

In this same canyon, some years later, a companion and I discovered an adult black-tailed rattlesnake sunning itself next to a bush. It had, like the juvenile in the preceding instance, evidently just crawled out from under a nearby rock—in this case a large chunk of granite—to take advantage of the first rays of the early morning sun.

Its only response to our approach was a flicking of the shiny black forked tongue.

I removed the dust cover from my camera and began to photograph the snake, which made no attempt to withdraw; nor did it offer to strike or even rattle. As I moved first to one side and then to the other the snake dutifully turned to face me. I became intrigued by its apparent ambivalence; docile and yet attentive to the slightest movement. I continued taking pictures, allowing the snake to become accustomed to my presence. Still it showed no concern.

I now reached out and placed the index finger of my left hand under the snake's chin, turning it slightly to the side. The snake offered not the slightest objection. I withdrew my hand and quickly snapped the picture.

Let me digress. It was spring, the year before I started college. The days were getting longer, and warmer. Cliff Hammond called. He wanted me to meet him at "Little Beaver Town," located just east of the city limits. He was there waiting for me.

As I arrived I could see him standing next to an old, ramshackle, shed with lots of boards and other building materials scattered around.

I got out of the old army jeep I was driving and shook his rather large hand. "It,s an old snake pit," Cliff told me. "This was part of an old tourist attraction."

The property had been purchased by Fred Harmen who writes the Little Beaver comic books. "He wants to turn it into an old western style amusement park and he's asked me to manage it.

"Let's take a look I said."

As we entered, it took a moment for my eyes to become accustomed to the dark. I could make out some rubble around what looked like it could have been a snake pit, about six feet by four feet and filled nearly to the top with boards and trash.

I jumped in and started to throw out the trash. About three feet down I could see the coil of a rattle snake. I tossed out another board. A snake struck, missing my boot by a good foot. That was enough for

Cliff. I had to get out, "You know, insurance rates and what not."

In a couple of days I had the place up and running. I brought in a half dozen cages and set up some displays, nothing fancy. I set a chair near the entrance and started accepting tickets, which could be purchased at the front gate.

This went rather well for a couple of weeks. Then it was explained to me that each night the park would put on a show, rotated among fourteen concessionaires. Tonight was my turn. Talk about short notice.

I called Lee Anderson and asked if he could help out. I wanted someone that I **knew** could handle poisonous snakes, on the outside chance that something went wrong.

I took out one of my transport cages, which has hardware cloth in front of the glass for protection. With my trusty hook, I removed a five foot diamondback from the pit, placed it in the cage and waited.

A stage was set up with seating for about fifty to one hundred spectators. I would regale them with my snake milking skills. Lee opened the cage and I gently lifted the rattlesnake and placed it on the stage. I pinned it with the rubber handle of my hook, then reached down and took a firm grasp at the sides of the snake's jaw. With my other hand, I removed a vial from my pocket, adroitly hooked one of the snake's fangs over the lip and squeezed the venom gland. I got several drops of venom. More than I had expected. Probably because the snake had not used any venom for nearly a year. I switched fangs and gave another squeeze. You could clearly see the honey colored venom running down the side of the tube. I replaced the snake in its cage and Lee closed the lid. I held the vial high for all to see. Blank stares. No reaction from the audience. Think fast What to do? I put the vial to my lips and tilting it skyward, swallowed. Yuk! It tasted like the inside of an old cave. Still blank stares.

As the audience filed out and we got ready to leave, I felt cliff's hand on my shoulder. Leaning forward, "How did you do that?" he asked.

In the spring of 1963 I was attending a class in herpetology at the University of New Mexico. Early in the morning of May 4, a small group of students met at the entrance of the biology building for a field trip to Los Lunas. It was warm and sunny, and everyone was filled with enthusiasm. A bus had been reserved from the motor pool and was now loaded with traps, preserving equipment and other necessary accouterments which come in handy on such occasions.

The leader of the expedition was our instructor, Dr. W. G. "Bill" Degenhardt, professor of herpetology at U. N. M. Accompanying us was an old friend and associate of Bill's, Carl Kauffeld. At the time, Carl was both Director and Curator of reptiles at New York's Staten Island Zoo.

Carl presented the character analyst with an interesting dichotomy of traits: both his professional stature and his personal demeanor indicated a certain dignity (he looked like he would be most comfortable in an English club), with a soft spoken air of authority; yet the most often mentioned memory of the trip, when discussed by participants, is Carl's sitting atop the bus in order to get a suntan! In short, his warmth and friendliness definitely added to our enjoyment of the trip, and his enthusiasm for field work was contagious.

Our first stop was a flooded field on the east side of the Rio Grande, just south of Isleta Pueblo. The bus pulled off the highway onto the soft sand at the shoulder of the road. There was a five or six-foot embankment between the highway and the field beyond. As I reached the top of the embankment, I noticed a small turtle sunning itself on a log in the middle of the field.

Now, I estimated that, at the place where the turtle was sunning itself, the water was about three feet deep. I also knew that the turtle would take alarm at my approach as soon as I entered the water, diving beneath the surface and disappearing amongst the grass and debris at the bottom.

I turned and walked back down the levee away from the turtle. Positioning myself across the highway, I ran toward the bank, gaining as much momentum as I could. I topped the bank and—with the added impetus of the down slope—was literally "flying" when I hit the water, which was all around me.

As expected, the turtle saw me coming. With one ambitious kick, the turtle hit the water—but it was too late.

I dove headlong into the water, groping for the turtle with both hands. I felt the shell, grabbed, and held on—the turtle kicking wildly. I lifted it triumphantly and waded back to shore—dripping wet.

We now proceeded across the river to the west side and on towards a lava formation known locally as "Los Lunas Mountain." Various members of the class managed to collect several interesting species to fulfill their course requirements. Among them were the western diamondback, coachwhip, bullsnake (or "gopher snake") and desert spiny lizard.

After lunch we drove back towards Albuquerque, stopping at the swamp east of Isleta Pueblo. Here we saw several common garter snakes and one lesser earless lizard. The day's collecting had been less than spectacular, but certainly enjoyable. On the return trip, Carl took the opportunity to joke with me about my innovative turtle-catching technique.

On a second trip, we decided to go farther south along the river to Bernardo, little more than a road junction and a filling station. This was an interesting area due to the contrasting habitats to be found in close proximity to one another.

On the east side of the highway, towards the river, was an irrigation canal. Beyond that was a grassy field containing a series of more or less permanent ponds. On the west side of the highway the Chihuahuan Desert exerted its influence. Clumps of vegetation (mostly mesquite and creosote) were widely separated, with expanses of sand between them. This looked like a likely habitat for leopard lizards, prairie rattlers and box turtles. Along the washes and gullies there were bushes that could provide cover for a variety of species.

While the others scattered out, mostly on the west side, I began slowly walking along the bank of the canal, keeping a sharp eye on the vegetation next to the water's edge. After about fifteen minutes of not seeing anything other than a few bullfrog tadpoles and a school of "guppies" (*Gambusia*), I decided to try my luck over in the field.

Cattails lined both sides of the road, providing excellent cover and nesting sites for red-winged blackbirds and boat-tailed grackles. The blackbirds, with their bright yellow and red wing patches and characteristic call, provide much of the charm of the swamp. On an early spring night one can hear the raucous calls of the tiny little chorus frogs. The sound produced is completely disproportionate to the size of the animal, and one at first imagines that the sound must be coming from an animal that is much larger.

Good fortune awaited me in the field. As I approached the first— and largest—pond, I could see patches of water here and there between the branches of vegetation at the water's edge. I walked very softly, as snakes are highly sensitive to ground vibrations. As I searched along the edge of the pond, my attention was drawn to something lying in the water just a little ways from the bank. It had dark scales with yellow centers. A kingsnake! A Sonora kingsnake, to be exact.

Kingsnakes are geographically variable. In California I have seen individuals with longitudinal stripes like those on garter snakes, while in Nevada I have collected members of the same species with alternating black and white bands. Here in the Rio Grande Valley the scales are black with varying degrees of yellow speckling, tending to form blotches down the center of the back. These are beautiful snakes and are considered a rarity in this area (although they tend to be somewhat more common farther south). This was a fortunate find, but I still had the problem of catching it.

In fact, the odds were distinctly in the snake's favor, as the branches made a stealthy approach inconceivable. The snake would certainly be warned of my presence and be out of sight amongst the aquatic vegetation. What to do?

Deciding that my best course of action would be the direct approach, I stood back a ways and then..."charged." I was sprawled out on the bank, my chest and arms in the water, groping for anything I could feel. My hands closed around a mixture of grass and algae. Had I missed? My disappointment soon turned to joy as I felt a prickling sensation in my fingers. Somewhere in the middle of all this "stuff" was a snake, chewing vigorously on my hand!

Later on that evening this snake would be added to the "live room" at the University—a welcome addition.

On yet another occasion, a friend and I were driving south on the old highway (U.S. 85) through the Isleta swamp just north of Los Lunas. We spied a snake on the road. It was just an ordinary bullsnake; nothing unusual about that. But there was something very odd about its behavior that attracted our attention.

The snake seemed completely unaware of our presence, so intent was it upon probing every square inch of the road's surface. It moved its head slowly from side to side, its forked tongue flicking frantically. What could it possibly be doing out here in the middle of the highway? We felt compelled to investigate.

As we approached, the snake ceased its probing, withdrawing its head slightly. We couldn't believe what we saw. Close inspection revealed a large scar across the top of the snake's head between the eyes. The scar itself was completely healed, but the eyes were missing. This snake was totally blind! It was, however, not totally helpless. It seemed to sense our direction and was obviously in a state of agitation. It appeared to be in otherwise perfect health.

On being touched it reacted violently. With a loud hiss, as only a bullsnake can hiss, it lashed out aggressively towards its tormentors. Of course, we had no intention of tormenting this unfortunate creature. Having crawled out onto the highway, it was unable to find any olfactory clues with which to orient itself. It was in a state of total confusion.

Getting it off the road presented a problem. It would not stay on the hook and steadfastly refused to retreat. Once we did manage to get it off the road, however, it seemed to be completely within its own element and, even more amazingly, seemed to know where it was going. We returned to our vehicle feeling like we had done our good deed for the day. It wasn't until later that we realized, in our eagerness to help the poor snake, neither of us had thought to take it's picture.

Dr. Charles M. Bogert, Curator Emeritus of the American Museum of Natural History, during a survey of reptiles and amphibians in Los Alamos county, New Mexico.

"Hippies picking mushrooms," author (L) and Bill Love (R), Sandoval County, N.M. Photo by Bill Love

Ted Brown preserves D.O.R.'s (Dead On Road), Grant Co., N.M. Ted is a pioneer of herpetology in New Mexico going back to his early teens.

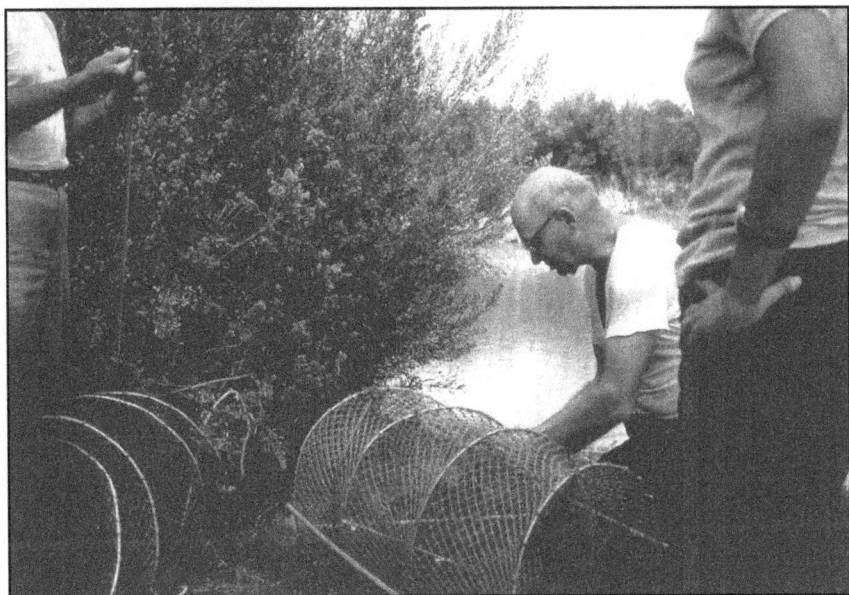

Roger Conant sets a turtle trap in the Rio Grande, Bernalillo Co., N.M. Dr. Conant is a contributing author to the Peterson field guide series. He was also a Professional Fellow of the A.A.Z.P A.

Spiny softshell turtle

Blacktail den, Bernalillo Co., New Mexico

Black-tailed rattlesnake

LUTHER

Late one night in October, 1962, I was standing in an unheated freight office at the Albuquerque International Airport, waiting to pick up a small reticulated python which had been shipped to me from an animal importer in Florida. The temperature outside was forty degrees Fahrenheit, and it could not have been much over fifty in the unheated room.

I paid the shipping charges and was handed a small box constructed of wood and Masonite, with a few small holes drilled in one end. The box measured approximately four by four by eight inches. I remember thinking at the time that they couldn't possibly fit a python, even a young one, into such a small box.

Inside the box was a cheesecloth sack. I untied the sack and gently poured its contents into the palm of my hand. It was a beautiful little snake—tiny, with big orange eyes. The black and gold "fishnet" pattern on a silver background was outstanding. The snake remained motionless, coiled in a tight ball. I cupped my hands, hoping that the warmth would elicit some sign of life. Finally, after several minutes, the tips of the forked tongue protruded, ever so slightly, from the notch in the snakes upper jaw. At least it was alive. I unzipped my coat and placed the still motionless reptile inside my shirt.

Arriving home, my immediate concern was for the health of the snake, which was still so cold it could hardly move. The big orange eyes with their black, elliptical pupils followed every movement, affording me some measure of encouragement. Movements of the tongue were now slow and deliberate.

I had prepared a cage for "him" (it later turned out to be a "her") that I hoped contained all the comforts necessary to maintain a healthy, happy python. The cage was four feet long, twelve inches deep and eighteen inches high. The cage temperature was thermostatically controlled to ensure that its occupant would not be exposed to drastic fluctuations in temperature—an absolutely essential precaution where tropical snakes are concerned. A large container of fresh water and a box into which the snake could retreat were placed in the cage along with a branch on which the snake could climb.

The snake was fed mice or young rats twice each week for the next three months. During this period its growth was phenomenal—three-sixteenths of an inch per day!

Luther, as *she* was called, soon became accustomed to people and readily accepted handling by me or others so long as it was done gently and there were no sudden movements. At no time did she ever offer to bite.

Luther continued to grow so that by the following summer it was necessary to build a larger cage. Instead of a branch I placed an elk antler in the cage. The antler was securely fastened in place to ensure against injuries. Nevertheless, even with these spacious accommodations she was spending more and more of her time wandering freely about the house in search of human companionship. When friends came by for a visit, Luther would join them on the sofa. Most of our friends adjusted to this state of affairs and a few actually seemed not to mind the inquisitive probings of a friendly tongue about their eyes and ears. This was just Luther's way of getting to know you; satisfied that she was among friends, she would wedge herself between two warm bodies or, as often as not, curl herself comfortably on an accommodating lap.

Her nemeses were twofold: ashtrays and coffee cups. and between the two, ashtrays were by far the worse—sending her into a sneezing fit that could last for several minutes. She would then continue making her rounds as if nothing had happened.

A tragedy was narrowly averted in one incident. I was feeding Luther some pigeons that I had trapped earlier in the day. Positioning myself before the open cage, I would throw in the pigeons one at a time. Luther would grab each pigeon in its turn, constrict and swallow (she always constricted, whether she was offered live food or not). One of the pigeons fell to the floor of the cage, unnoticed. I should have realized what would follow, but this was so routine I wasn't paying much attention.

As I reached in to retrieve the pigeon, Luther (mistaking my hand for food) made a sudden grab, sinking all of her three-hundred-odd teeth into the metacarpal region. She simultaneously threw several stout coils around my forearm, drawing my head and right shoulder into the cage and pinning me against the elk antler.

Aside from being embarrassed, I was concerned that in extricating myself I might cause injury to the snake. Relaxing my arm, I resigned myself to whatever might happen next. I was absolutely sure of only one thing: there was no way that an eleven foot python was going to swallow a one-hundred-sixty-pound man.

Luther soon realized her error, released her grip and slid apologetically (if I may be allowed to anthropomorphize just a little) to the floor. Feeding was resumed without further incident

It soon became apparent that even this cage was not going to be big enough for very long. By the end of her third summer, Luther was fully thirteen feet long and **still** growing! (She was by now eating full grown chickens and even an occasional rabbit).

This time I built a large cage which occupied most of one end of the dining room. It had an all-glass front, with a shelf at one end and the elk antler and water dish at the other. It was sanded and finished to blend with the decor of the room.

Luther was not happy. No matter how comfortable and accommodating this new cage, she simply did not like being shut up. She prowled continuously about the cage, probing first one corner and then another, seeking a way out. Finally she refused to feed, and after several long weeks I relented.

Luther was her old self again, happily roaming about the house, greeting visitors, knocking over lamps, dumping ashtrays, and having all manner of fun. So accustomed were we to her presence that we often neglected to mention her to unfamiliar folk, an oversight which at times created quite a stir. I recall the time we were visited by two salesman. I never even had an opportunity to inquire as to the nature of their goods or services. They started to say something about a survey they were conducting and then, in their haste to get to their next appointment, they just left—*through* the screen door (without opening it). The entire door had to be replaced.

On one occasion while I had Luther out for some exercise on the front lawn, my father stopped by for a visit. As we stood talking, Luther crawled over to us and, raising the forepart of her body (and after the proper inspection), laid her chin on his shoulder. My father went right on with his conversation as if nothing had happened. Actually, he was used to this sort of thing, as Luther would quite often pick him out of a group. Perhaps she liked the smell of his brand of tobacco, I don't know, but I think it was probably because he always moved slowly and never acted startled or nervous.

Luther was tolerant of small children as well as adults. After suffering the indignity of having her tail pulled, she would sometimes register her mild disapproval by retreating behind the sofa. Before long, however, her head would reappear over the top of the sofa and, after satisfying herself that the situation was again under control, she would emerge, tongue wagging, her old congenial self.

After talking it over, Mabel and I decided that, all things considered, Luther would probably be better off in a zoo. Not just any zoo, however. I sent a letter off to Carl Kauffeld at the Staten Island Zoo in New York explaining my predicament. Here, certainly, she would be in good hands.

Carl had heard just about every snake story that had ever been told, and conceded that Luther must certainly be an unusual animal. After calling Bill Degenhardt to confirm the snake's condition and temperament, he proposed to the Zoo's Board of Directors that I be compensated three hundred dollars for my investment, which I felt was more than generous. And so it was final. The date was set for the shipment of Luther.

According to Carl, Luther was approaching the twenty-foot mark at the time of her death in 1968.

Luther, although just a snake, exhibited a marked preference for human companionship. For a nonsocial animal this is somewhat remarkable in itself. But she was also a pet in the best sense of the word as I know it. Although there will always be skeptics, there are undeniably aspects of animal behavior for which there is currently no explanation.

RAMSEY

Late in the summer of 1963, I had just finished reading Carl Kauffeld's book, "Snakes and Snake Hunting," for the third or even fourth time. As I lay my head back and closed my eyes, I conjured up visions of secluded canyons where shadowy leaf-littered floors and steep rocky slopes abounded in all manner of marvelous creatures waiting to be discovered. What I wouldn't have give then to be hiking up the trail to the "Hamburg Mine," climbing the talus on "Onion Saddle" or "cruising" the "Ajo Road."

Of all the places mentioned in Carl's book, probably none is more familiar among snake hunters than the Huachuca Mountains, located in south-central Arizona along the international boundary between the United States and Mexico.

By coincidence, my brother Bruce was living in southern Arizona at the time, working as a technical writer at Fort Huachuca. You can imagine my excitement when he invited me to spend two weeks at his home in Sierra Vista, only fifteen minutes away by car from the Huachuca Mountains. I was packed and waiting the following morning when my brother arrived.

It was after dark when we pulled into Lordsburg. Thunderclouds rolled across the darkened sky, boding tough weather ahead.

Rain poured down over the windshield of my brother's '57 Chevrolet. I knew from experience that summer thunderstorms are a common occurrence on the desert, but I myself had never witnessed anything like this before!

As Bruce and I peered ahead through the darkness, we could foresee little relief from the incessant deluge. We decided to take the southern route through Bisbee rather than continue on west to Benson and then south to Sierra Vista.

As we crossed over the Peloncillos, the rain intensified. The windshield wipers beat frantically but futilely. We rolled down the windows and stuck our heads outside, struggling to see the blacktop highway ahead of us. There came a loud crack of thunder. The smell of ozone filled the air. Lightening flashed all around us now.

We proceeded cautiously. Consulting our well-worn copy of Rand McNally, we made the necessary adjustments in our course and were soon headed west—towards Benson.

To our relief the rain seemed to subside, but did not entirely stop even as we approached Sierra Vista. This was great weather for spadefoot toads, and these little "gnomes of the night" made their presence known in great profusion. To the casual observer they may have at first appeared to be nothing more than a scattering of pebbles in the roadway—that is, until their animate nature revealed itself in a brief burst of short hops. These little toads take their name from a horny, spade-like structure on the hind foot which is used for burrowing backwards into the ground.

Spadefoot tadpoles are voracious predators—even cannibalistic, a necessary strategy for survival in the desert. Breeding is opportunistic, and what little water is available may only last for a few days. The little tadpoles must metamorphosis quickly, or not at all. To do this requires a plentiful supply of protein. What better source could they find? Spadefoot toads are prolific breeders, and many more of the species are born than could ever hope to survive; this is certainly true of most amphibians, spadefoots being no exception. Thus, some must perish that others might live.

To my delight there now appeared in our headlights the lumbering form of a Colorado River toad making its way, somewhat awkwardly, across the road.

As Bruce applied the brakes, I jumped out with a handy minnow bucket in which to contain my intended catch. The toad had other ideas. As I knelt down to place the bucket over him, he made a casual hop to one side, just out of reach. Bruce came to the rescue with a hand net, and we managed to subdue our quarry without further ado.

Arriving at my brother's apartment shortly after 1:00 a.m., we hurriedly unloaded our gear and, serenaded by spadefoot toads and lulled by the slow but steady rain, were soon sleeping soundly.

I spent the following day reconnoitering the area on a bicycle. Five miles east of town was the San Pedro River. Here skinks and whiptail lizards abound. To my great satisfaction, I surprised a large coachwhip snake which had made a determined effort to conceal itself beneath a piece of corrugated tin. The body was salmon pink, with a black head and black bands on the neck, characteristic of the "piceus" subspecies. It made no attempt to bite, but struggled to free itself when restrained. I released it and began making my way slowly back towards town.

The next day, Saturday, Bruce and I decided to drive up into Ramsey Canyon, the northernmost of several major canyons in the Huachuca range which open eastward overlooking the San Pedro River valley. We had driven several miles into the canyon when the pavement abruptly ended. From here on the road deteriorated rapidly. We passed a small monument dedicating Ramsey Canyon as a registered national landmark.

"Private property" signs now lined both sides of the road. A sharp bend brought us up with finality to a metal gate. The sign on the gate read, "Private property KEEP OUT." A chain was wrapped around the gatepost and on it hung an open padlock.

Leaving the car, we opened the gate; then, closing it securely behind us, began slowly walking up the driveway towards the first of several buildings. They were constructed of darkly-stained timbers with pitched corrugated metal roofs and were partially concealed by vegetation. They seemed very old, but well kept.

An assortment of small dogs greeted us noisily. The house was occupied by Bill and Nell Brown, caretakers for the property which was owned by N. C. Bledsoe, a pioneer doctor of the area, then residing in Tucson.

When I first saw Bill, who was retired from the Border Patrol, he was sitting on the concrete steps leading up to the house. He wore a khaki shirt and trousers, and on his head was a wide-brimmed felt hat, pushed back from his forehead. My first impression was that of an individual who had spent a great deal of time outdoors and who, by the looks of him, had weathered more than just a few "storms" in his time.

In spite of what we perceived as a general distrust for strangers, after the first round of introductions (during which he let Nell do most of the talking, while he primarily observed) Bill seemed to warm to us. Intruders, we were told, were commonplace—and most of them showed little respect for the natural beauty of the mountain. We learned that hundreds of people visit the canyon annually, most of them collectors— be it snakes, birds' eggs, bottles or bugs (the latter two of which were also Nell's interests).

After securing permission, Bruce and I returned to our car and began preparations for our hike up the canyon. We traveled light, carrying only the obligatory canteens, snake bags and one hook.

I led the way up the steep firebreak and then back down to the stream. A natural dike transects the trail here to form the "box." The *Equisetum*, or "horsetail," grew waist high and was still covered with morning dew. Stands of New Mexico locust were so thick that they nearly obscured the stream in some places. At my feet I noticed a large, orange-colored mushroom with white "scales"; this I recognized as the deadly *Amanita muscaria*.

Instead of following the trail I decided to leave the stream bed at this point, a fortuitous decision as it turned out, that would bring me eventually to the "reef" above Carr Canyon, the next big canyon to the south.

I made my way around the outcrop of rocks, my hands slipping on the wet moss. There was so much moisture in the air that by now our clothing had become damp.

The climb to the top was long and arduous. As we made our way between two ridges, the loose talus beneath our feet made climbing all the more difficult. Nearer the top, dense stands of Manzanita tore at our clothes. Straining now to catch our breath but too excited to stop for a rest, we continued climbing until we reached the reef.

Lepidus! I could hardly believe my eyes. There on a little shelf of rock, not three feet from my right knee, was the most beautiful little black and green banded rattlesnake I had ever seen. By this time Bruce (who was carrying the bags) had caught up with me. And by this time, too, the snake—realizing our presence—had begun to "sing"; still it did not move. It must have felt secure, concealed as it was against the green lichen-encrusted rocks. Here was a snake not at all reluctant to rattle and yet unwilling to make the slightest movement. It must instinctively understood that any movement, however slight, would in an instant render useless that marvelous cryptic pattern with which nature, in its wisdom, had seen fit to endow it.

We moved slowly now, searching every crack in the rocks, every crevice. Bzzzzzz! A second "green rock," this one about eighteen inches long, a little larger than the first. Both were males. By now it was 1:30 p.m., and we were both ready for a break. We rested for the better part of an hour. Then, following the game trails, we began working our way back down the mountain.

Walking briskly, I again took the lead while Bruce followed with the bag containing the snakes. At one point the trail was so steep that Bruce was actually above me. As I passed a fallen log, I noticed a sudden movement. The snake was crawling almost at my heel and buzzing like fury. My first thought was that there must be a hole in the sack; surely this was no place for any rock rattlesnake to be. A quick check, however, showed our former captives were safe and secure. We had been out less than three hours and already had three handsome rock rattlesnakes.

The following weekend, Nell and her daughter Ruth offered to hike up the canyon with me. Bruce, still sore from the previous hike, decided to sit this one out. This time, instead of following the fire break, we went up through the box.

Here the walls of the canyon are so close you can almost reach out and touch both sides at once. A clear mountain stream cascades over polished rocks, here and there forming crystal pools in the limestone basins. One must walk with great deliberation over the slippery rocks. Orchids and other wild flowers grow in abundance. As we passed, a canyon treefrog, clinging to the rocks with specialized toe pads, released his grip and splashed headlong into the stream, disappearing beneath the ripples.

We now came to the spot where the fire break crosses the stream. Yarrow's spiny lizards scampered from rock to rock as we passed, their iridescent red and green bodies sparkling like jewels in the sunlight.

We continued upstream, crisscrossing it not less than eleven times before coming to the trail that leads over a saddle into Carr Canyon. Here dense stands of long-needle pines cast dark shadows on the canyon floor. The women, stopping now and then to admire a hummingbird or butterfly, had fallen a little distance behind. I followed the trail for about twenty-five yards and then sat down on a log to wait for the others.

As I waited, a band-tailed pigeon, maneuvering skillfully through the branches, landed on a limb above my head. He did not seem disturbed by my presence and I watched him for several minutes. I happened to glance down at my feet; and there, stretched out next to the log, was a twin-spotted rattlesnake! A very rare snake in the Huachucas, *Crotalus pricei* is considered to be somewhat more common in the Chiricahua Mountains, some sixty miles to the northeast (as the crow flies). This was not an especially large snake, even fore a twin-spot, which usually do not grow to be over two feet. But what a snake which is usually associated with talus was doing in a place like this was certainly a puzzle.

Reluctant to "pin" such a small and delicate snake as this, I reached down and gently lifted it with my hook. With my free hand I removed one of the muslin sacks from my belt loop. Gingerly I guided the snake into the bag. What a find!

By now Nell and her daughter had caught up to me. We continued walking up the canyon. To our left, Carr Peak towered above us. A black-chinned hummingbird hovered for an instant then darted off and disappeared among the trees.

We came to an old smelter which had been partially destroyed by vandals, presumably for the "Hamburg" bricks, which are something of a collector's item. Old timbers and sheets of rusted tin were strewn over the ground. On our right was an old mine shaft with its associated talus.

The clouds were moving in and there was a good chance we were all going to get wet. With the little snake safe and secure in its sack, however, I didn't mind. The cloudburst hit as we were coming within sight of the house. Laughing, we ran to reach the shelter of the porch. "This is nothing unusual," Nell told me. "In the last two weeks, we've had over an inch and a quarter of rain."

We spent the remainder of the afternoon looking at Bill's mineral collection and watching the many varieties of hummingbirds that took refuge under the eaves of the porch. Bill then offered to drive me into town to save Bruce the trip out.

As we drove, Bill told me all about the history of the canyon. I listened quietly, taking mental notes, as he talked of his experiences working with the Border Patrol in the early days, when Tombstone (not Bisbee) was the county seat. I glanced back over my shoulder, bidding a silent farewell to the Huachucas and to my newfound friends in Ramsey Canyon. Bruce and I were soon on our way back to New Mexico, but I was determined to return to this paradise in the desert.

Twin-spotted rattlesnake

Arizona alligator lizard

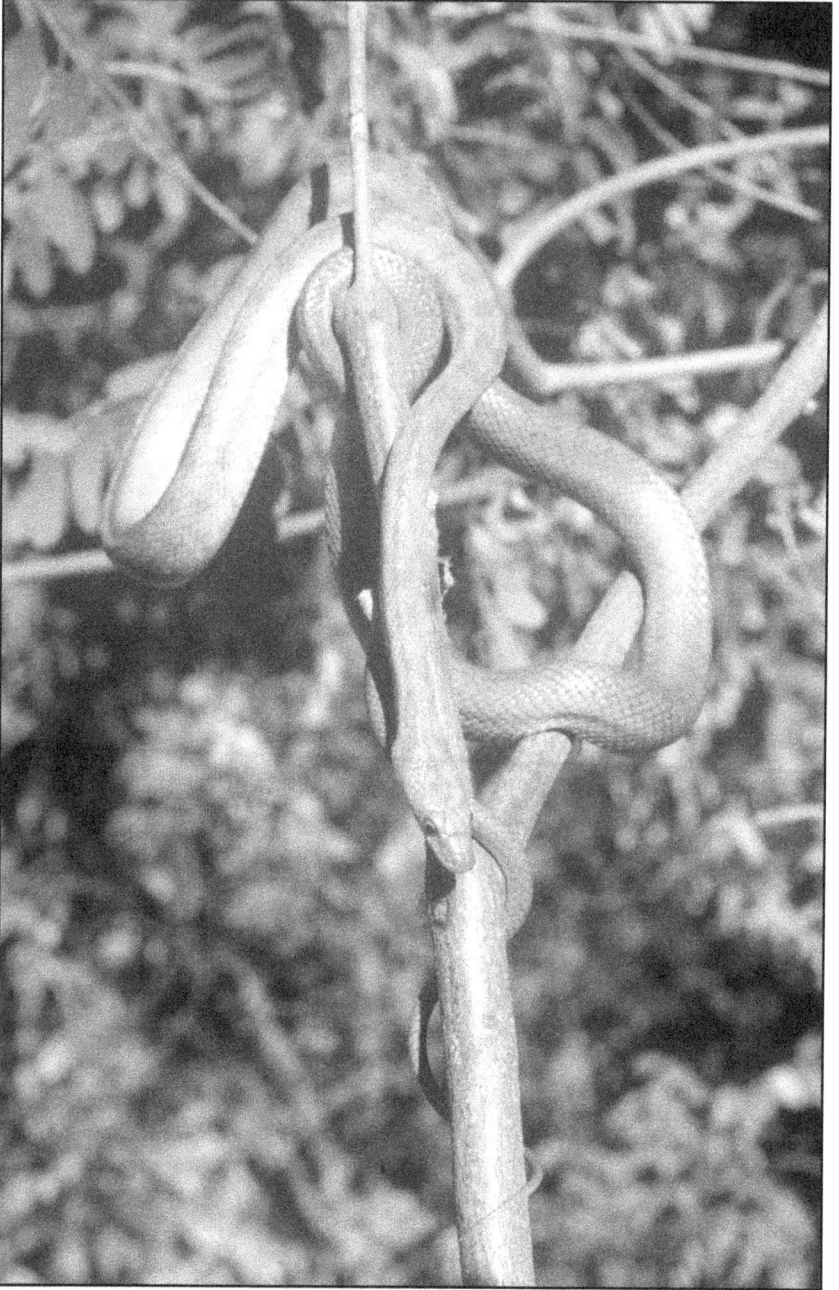

Green rat snake

RETURN TO RAMSEY

Paradise is about three miles northwest of Portal, Arizona, which (as the crow flies) is not more than five miles west of Rodeo (pronounced "rho-DAY-oh"), which, in turn, is fourteen miles from Animas by way of Antelope Pass, which is some thirty miles due south of Lordsburg, which can be found on any road map. Both Paradise and Portal are nestled in the foothills of the Chiricahua Mountains, which is where this story begins.

For Mabel and me this was to be our honeymoon—the first of more than a dozen trips that we would make together to southern Arizona over the next decade or so. No matter what else we did, we always paid a visit to Nell Brown in Ramsey Canyon.

We arrived at Onion Saddle in late afternoon. We had stopped by the American Museum's Southwest Research Station on the way up and the museum director suggested this would be a likely spot to find twin-spotted rattlesnakes. This was considered one of the common rattlesnakes in these mountains at that time.

The sky was cloudy and it looked like we might get some rain. We pitched our tent and ate a quick supper. As there was still plenty of daylight left, I decided to examine the extensive talus, the base of which was almost in our camp. I began making my way towards the top. Sheer cliffs defined the upper limits of the talus, denying access to the top. I made my way slowly along the base of the cliff, detouring from time to time around a stand of scrub oak which had taken a foothold near the edge of the rocks. All the while I kept a sharp eye out for the small gray-colored rattlesnake with the double row of brown spots, aligned one row on each side of the dorsal mid-line, from which this elusive little snake takes its name.

This was perfect habitat for these snakes. I recalled how surprised I'd been the previous summer in Ramsey to find the same species, totally unexpectedly, in quite different surroundings.

I moved slowly, almost on my hands and knees, peering into even the most insignificant cranny. To my ears came a faint buzzing sound, betraying the presence of a well-concealed rattlesnake. I stopped to listen. Yes, it very definitely was a snake.

I lifted first one rock...then another, being very careful so as not to inadvertently start a slide, which could very possibly injure the snake. The sound was deceptive—seemingly so close, and yet so faint as to be almost inaudible. Then, there it was, lying partially concealed between two rocks. It was a sub-adult. Now the dilemma: no way to pin it.

To attempt to do so would only cause it to slip down into the talus where it would quickly disappear. I slid my right hand around behind and beneath the snake, hoping to block its retreat. With my free hand I very carefully moved the rock against which it was resting. He dropped right into my hand. He had cease his rattling, and began to look about at my fingers. "Trying to figure out which one to bite," I imagined.

I quickly dropped him into one of the muslin sacks Mabel had made for me. These were custom stitched across the corners to ensure that a snake would not become entangled trying to escape.

I called to Mabel. "Got one," I said, holding up the bag. The clouds were darkening as I made my way quickly down the slope. We slept soundly through the night, awakening only occasionally to the sound of raindrops falling gently against the canvas tent.

The sky was still overcast when we awoke the following morning. Everything was soaking wet from the rain. We packed our belongings into the jeep and headed towards Portal. Mabel spied a female black bear at the base of a large pine tree just a few yards off the road. Camera in hand, she climbed down from the jeep and prepared to take its picture. Only then did we notice the two cubs still up in the tree. With a loud grunt the female turned and started down the hill. One of the cubs followed, but the other seemed to be having a bit of difficulty extricating itself from the tanglement of branches. A loud squeal from the frightened cub brought the mother bear, who spun around on her heels and headed straight towards us. She didn't even slow down as she passed the tree. She just kept right on coming.

The jeep began to roll forward; slowly at first, then gradually gaining momentum. Mabel forgot all about her picture. Tossing the camera in ahead of her, she tumbled into the jeep. Away we went, with the bear in hot pursuit. Satisfied that we were no longer a threat, she returned to her cubs, none the worse for wear—and luckily, neither were we.

The next stop was Ramsey Canyon. Perhaps this time, I thought, I would be lucky enough to find the rarest rattlesnake of all; a small snake, less than two feet long, the rust color of fallen oak leaves and the white facial markings were enough to distinguish this snake from all others. But the most unique feature was the ridge, running all the way around the upper margin of the snout, and formed by the raised canthal scales—a feature shared with no other species of rattlesnake.

We arrived at the browns' house after midnight; the lights were out. The darkness surrounding the house was increased by its presence in the canyon and the enclosing large trees, as well as there being no moon out.

As I groped my way walking up the drive, I heard the dogs rattling their feed pans. I wondered why they didn't bark, since they usually raise quite a ruckus. I assumed they were more inclined to finish off their dinners. As I stepped up onto the porch, the dogs crowded around me in greeting.

I had started to knock, but then, as the hairs slowly began to rise on the back of my neck, I suddenly recognized another sound coming from the uncharacteristically quiet "dogs" around me. The peculiar snorting and snapping jaws were unmistakable sounds of only one animal I knew; javelina!

Not wanting to tangle with those three-to-four inch tusks (or the unpredictable behavior for which javelina are justifiably renowned), I slowly backed my way down off the porch and over to the jeep.

Once safely inside, I explained to Mabel that there had been a change of plans and we would be spending the night in the jeep. When I related my guess about the number (eighteen or twenty) and, more relevantly, the kind of animals on the porch, she readily agreed to our change in sleeping quarters.

The next morning I asked Nell why the dogs hadn't been barking the night before when we arrived. She explained that they're always quiet when the javelina are around, because they're hiding under the bed. She went on to say that the javelina came around because she had fed the babies during the last cold winter, and they had no fear of people as a result. Then she announced that she had a surprise for us.

On the coffee table rested a gallon jar with some holes punched in the lid and filled with wadded-up tissue paper. Nell reached into the jar and pulled out a beautiful red, yellow and black banded snake. It wasn't a large snake, only about two feet long, with a black mask over its eye and a yellow nose. It was a mountain kingsnake. I was speechless. She laid the snake in my hand. Needless to say, it became one of my most prized possessions. She had found it out by the barn—right in her own front yard.

It was too late to hike up the canyon by the time we finished recounting the events of the past year, so we contented ourselves with pitching camp down by the gate and making preparations for an early start in the morning. I remember thinking that the only thing more exciting to find than a ridge-nose would be a green rat snake, but surely this would be asking for a little too much, as these snakes were not known to occur in this range of mountains.

The following morning we were up early as usual. We had our standard camp breakfast of boiled eggs and crackers. With canteens, bags and snake hook, we began the long trek up the mountain. Mabel opted for the fire break, while I stayed in the canyon. As I reached the place where the fire break crosses the stream, I heard Mabel calling.

"I saw a rattlesnake up on the hill," she said.

"What kind?"

"A rock rattler."

"Let's go!"

Mabel was ahead of me, pointing the way to where she had seen the small greenish-gray snake with dark velvet cross-bands. "I think it went into that hole;" she pointed to an opening between two rocks. I knelt down and put my ear to the opening. I could hear a faint rattling sound, but I couldn't tell just where it was coming from. Carefully I lifted one of the rocks, laying it to one side to be replaced later.

Still I could see no snake. I began cautiously to move the second rock. All the while I could hear the faint rattling sound. Curiously, it didn't seem to be getting any closer.

"There it is," Mabel said, pointing to an exposed Manzanita root not six inches from where I had turned over the first rock! The little snake, little more than a foot long, was lying there in the shadow of the root. It had blended in so perfectly that I had completely overlooked it, even though it was close enough that it probably could have bitten me; although I doubted that the bite of such a small snake would have been very serious.

Mabel sat down to catch her breath; it was a steep hike up the firebreak. She had made a remarkable find—again in what seemed to us to be an unlikely location; a phenomenon to which we were becoming more and more accustomed. The rule seems to be: "Expect snakes where you find them, when they are there."

I sat back to admire the little rattler, a young female. Here was something no one else had ever seen. Others like it, certainly, but not this particular individual. I pondered releasing it for a while, and then decided (since it was Mabel's first rock rattlesnake), to keep it. I then began to photograph our prize, as Mabel looked on triumphantly.

We continued upstream past the point of rocks, pushing our way through the large stand of New Mexico locust, taking care to avoid its sharp thorns. We stopped to check out a small talus on the left slope, then went on. We had crossed the stream, we counted, eleven times before we reached the point where the trail divides and, beyond that, the "meadow." This is the same "rocky glade" that Kauffeld refers to in his book, "Snakes and Snake Hunting."

In the center of the meadow stood a corner post and broken-down fence rails of the "old corral," a well-known landmark to seekers of mountain-dwelling rattlesnakes in these parts. This was the same corral as Carl Kauffeld talks about, as I recall; although Carl had come in over the ridge from Carr Canyon—a somewhat longer, though less demanding hike.

Two men were standing near the corral as we arrived. They were dressed in cowboy outfits, each with a pack on his back and a six gun on his hip. "An unnecessary over-dramatization," I remember thinking to myself. They were, so they said, from California, having just arrived at the spot a few moments ahead of us. We mutually agreed to part company, Mabel and I taking the trail over the saddle towards Sunnyside.

We had hiked for over an hour. Then, after a short rest, decided to try our luck back at the meadow. I led the way, Mabel following, as we hiked leisurely along the narrow, leaf strewn path. The sun was high overhead, filtering down through the branches of tall pine trees. As I walked, I was struck by the myriad of mushrooms; they came in all sizes and colors. Here and there were clumps of a small, yellow species belonging to the genus *Collybia*—quite palatable, or so I am told. Also plentiful was the solitary form, much like an eel's head, rising out of the soil; this was a "stinkwart."

Mabel had caught up and was walking beside me. "Look," she cried. There in the path, not two feet beyond where I was standing, was the most beautiful black-tailed rattlesnake I have ever seen, boldly patterned with velvet black markings on a golden yellow ground color. It lay motionless, coiled and partially concealed in the grass and leaf litter. This was the exact spot we had passed not more than half an hour earlier.

Only an occasional flick of its black tongue indicated that the snake was aware of us. I instinctively swung my camera into position. This was a real beauty. I moved in close, but still the snake did not move.

Mabel prodded it gently with the hook. It began to move—slowly, cautiously, probing the air nervously—but still, no rattle. I took several more pictures. We left the snake where we had found it, lying in its spot of sun on the trail.

It wasn't long until we reached the meadow. A flicker flew across the clearing ahead of us. Flashes of brick red on the under surface of its wings, coupled with the characteristic undulating flight, made this species easily recognized, even in flight.

We arrived at the meadow to find that we were alone; there was no sign of the "intruders." Mabel wanted to get a picture of me standing by the corral. "How's this," I asked, placing my hand on the fence post. "Its my turn to take your picture now," I said, starting towards her.

I hardly got the words out of my mouth, however, before we were startled by a high pitched "buzzzz." The distinctive rattle was certainly not that of a black-tail. I looked down to see a blur of rust colored scales as the snake, moving with alacrity through the tall grass, attempted to escape into a hole beneath the post.

Realizing it was about to get away, I dove, grasping the snake at mid-body. I still could not believe what I held in my hand—my first ridge-nosed rattlesnake—the rarest rattlesnake in the United States! For a long moment I just stared at the snake, which continued to rattle furiously but made no attempt to bite.

I removed a muslin bag from my belt loop and slid my newfound prize gently into it. Mabel shared my enthusiasm as she gazed with disbelief down into the bag. I took one last glance into the sack. The white flash-markings on the face and the ridge of raised scales around the margin of the snout left no room for doubt about the critter's identity. It was an adult male, fully two feet long and recently shed.

The clouds were moving in now and getting darker. We would have to hurry if we were going to get back before the rain started.

As we walked, my thoughts returned to the small snake in the bag. In certain respects the resemblance of the ridge-nosed rattlesnake to the copperhead of the southeastern United States is remarkable, both in morphology and life-style—an analogy first mentioned by Kauffeld in his book.

Both snakes show a preference for riparian habitats, with at least seasonal availability of surface water. There are other similarities in habitat, as well. Likewise both species tend to be somewhat unspecialized in their feeding habits, accepting a wide assortment of food items, including both warm and cold blooded prey—vertebrates and (especially in the young) invertebrates alike. In a study written for the Bureau of Land Management, John Applegarth also pondered the significance of the dark pigment under the chin, another character both species have in common. The metallic colors, ridged canthals and prominent facial striping are all features shared by both the ridge-nosed rattlesnake and the copperhead.

At least some of these similarities may be considered conservative, indicative of a common ancestry. The rattlesnakes are, after all, "pit vipers," and *Crotalus willardi* is undeniably an ancient member of the group. There are remarkable differences as well, which may be of equal phylogenetic significance. One puzzling fact is that, while all members of the genus *Agkistrodon* to which the copperheads belong, have large head shields, the head of the ridge-nosed rattlesnake is covered by small, granular scales. To further complicate the issue of phylogenetic relationships, another genus of rattlesnakes, the so called "pigmy rattlers," also exhibits large head shields.

As Lawrence Klauber points out, however, scale morphology is certainly not as conservative a feature as one might suspect. Klauber also points out that this variable is highly susceptible to environmental influences during ontogenetic development—at least experimentally. It is also possible that some of the noted similarities are the result of convergent evolution—a consequence of specialization to like habitats.

The purpose of the pit as a heat sensor has long been known. Various tests over the years demonstrate its sensitivity to infrared radiation (heat). This function of the pit was first described by G. Kingsley Noble in the 1930's.

The way snakes process and ultimately make use of information perceived by these specialized organs has eluded researchers until recently, however. Peter H. Hartline and his colleagues have done extensive background research into the mechanism of this unique sensory system with some rather impressive results.

Hartline and Eric A. Newman, of the Eye Research Institute in Boston, using some skillfully designed investigative techniques, have been able to show that in at least two families of snakes (Viperidae and Boidae) the infrared and visible light messages are integrated in the brain to yield a unique wide-spectrum picture of the world. Not surprisingly, this integration takes place on the optic tectum of the midbrain; a structure traditionally associated with vision and instrumental in an organism's spatial interpretation of its external environment.

The investigators concluded that a selective advantage would be conferred upon nocturnal or cave adapted forms possessing such thermoreceptors and feeding on warm blooded prey, as the primary function seems to be that of guiding the snake's strike.

Just how snakes use their infrared capabilities—whether or not they use their infrared detectors during the day, or whether they rely on their detectors to identify prey or perhaps locate a comfortable resting place—continues to be a source of conjecture. What is known is that the infrared neuronal connectivity pattern in pythons represents the most complex somatic connectivity scheme observed for any animal to date.

Garth Underwood, in *"A Contribution to the Classification of Snakes,"* has conclusively demonstrated the conservative nature of the pit genome in the phylogenetic history of the boas and pythons, a phenomenon which underscores the need for adaptive flexibility between the organism and its environment. Underwood argues convincingly, "real `characters' shared within a group are in fact manifestations of a `competence' to exhibit that particular phenotype, elicited by an evocator." This would seem to indicate that even an organ system as complex as that of the pits of certain snakes can appear and reappear over and over within a phylogenetic line.

The question of phylogenetic relationships, though largely academic, in no way diminishes the aesthetic appreciation that one inevitably feels for the snake, especially when encountered in nature. Essence, like beauty, is in the eye of the beholder and, to me, every living species is a marvel in its own right—a source of joy and wonderment.

Meanwhile, nightfall found us back on the Brown's veranda. The thunder rumbled and crashed with a vengeance around us; the rain poured down, filling the stream to its banks. This, in typical desert fashion, would go on until the early hours of the morning. I recalled that "Huachuca" is an old Indian word meaning "mountain of storms."

I reached out and picked up the sack containing the young female rock rattlesnake we had collected on the fire trail. To my genuine astonishment, when I opened the bag, I discovered not one, but five little lepidus—the original female and four miniature replicas.

The next morning I was up with the sun, anxious to get going. After the excitement of the previous day, Mabel had decided to stay behind and do some sight-seeing. As I hiked up through the box I spotted a patch of freshly turned earth. "Javelina," I thought to myself.

Everything was wet from the rain. Even the moss on the rocks seemed to have new life. The stream was running higher than before, making navigation of the box difficult. It was taking longer to warm up this morning. The Yarrow's spiny lizards were out, trying to catch the first rays of the early morning sun.

As I approached the firebreak I noticed a section of rail, no doubt left over from a more active period in the history of the Hamburg, when heavily laden ore carts pulled by mules were a common sight.

For no particular reason, I knelt down and turned it over with my hand. I was surprised to see a small lizard lying motionless beneath the rail. It appeared to be made of glass, so shiny were its scales. The body was olive-tan above, the tail had a distinctly purplish tint, and there was a light stripe just above the eye, extending back over the shoulder. This was a mountain skink, coiled in a tight semicircle and making no attempt to escape—a behavior I had come to associate with these extremely agile lizards.

My continued presence had apparently become a source of annoyance to the skink, however, as it now turned to face me. It was only then that I discovered the answer to its perplexing behavior—several small, whitish ovals partially buried in a depression, heretofore concealed from view. A female with eggs! I remember thinking this was a little late in the season for eggs. Not wishing to disturb them, I carefully replaced the rail

Unlike most lizards, the mother skink, having laid her eggs (usually under a rock or log), does not abandon them. She will remain to protect them until they hatch. Should a heavy rain inundate the "nest," she will bury the eggs. Or, if the ground becomes too dry, she may dig them up and move them to a more suitable location. Should an egg inadvertently roll out of the nest, she will retrieve it. She may even borrow eggs from an unattended neighboring clutch.

I paused briefly to inspect a small talus, the same one where Mabel and I had stopped yesterday. The canopy was less open here and the steep incline of the trail told me that I would soon reach the meadow. I proceeded towards a low hill covered with a scattering of good-sized rocks. This seemed to be as good a place as any to start looking; for what I wasn't quite sure. Its this element of suspense that makes the quest so interesting.

I turned the first rock. A long, slender and distinctly-banded figure darted out and disappeared beneath the rock next to it. Having difficulty making out any identifiable form, I lifted the rock slightly. I could just see the tail.

Reaching beneath the rock, I carefully placed my hand over the now struggling reptile and felt its smooth, shiny scales against my palm. With my left hand I forced back the rock. I had to be very gentle for this was an alligator lizard belonging to the family Anguidae, a highly specialized group of lizards which includes the "glass snakes" and which have the disconcerting habit of voluntarily discarding their caudal element at the slightest provocation; they simply drop off their tails. This bit of distraction has survival value, as you can imagine, for the tail continues to wriggle in somewhat violent fashion for several minutes. Any predator thus distracted will, more often than not, allow the tail's owner (or should I say "former owner"?) to make good his escape.

Special muscles in the base of the tail constrict to close off blood vessels so the abbreviated lizard does not bleed to death. The lizard will eventually grow a new tail—a process known as "regeneration"—

although it may not have exactly the same texture and color as the original. This one was a fine specimen, almost six inches long.

Turning a few more rocks and, incidentally, always taking care to replace them, I was fortunate to find another of the same species. This one was a juvenile, even more conspicuously banded than the first. After several more minutes of searching I was rewarded with the discovery of yet a third, larger than either of the first two and quick to take refuge under an old plank. Now matter how careful one tries to be, accidents will happen. Lifting the plank, I found this handsome lizard and its tail had already parted company. I made no effort to pursue it.

I continued the hunt, following up one of the many side canyons. Large boulders protruded from the leaf litter, almost knee-deep in places. As I turned my head I saw a small figure perched atop one of the boulders—a lizard. But not just any lizard—this was a bunch grass lizard, a diminutive relative of the somewhat larger and less graceful Yarrow's spiny lizard. The distinctive pattern of alternating yellow and lavender stripes told me this was a female, and the elongated bulges along her sides indicated she was gravid and very close to laying.

At my approach she dropped to the ground and darted behind the rock, only to reappear on the other side. Maintaining as low a profile as possible, I inched forward cautiously to within arm's reach. Wriggling the fingers of one hand to distract her attention, I made a grab with the other. I took only one photograph and then released her.

As I proceeded farther, the canyon narrowed. I passed a large talus on the left and made a mental note to check it on the way back. Moving along at a fairly brisk pace I came upon an old miner's shack. This was obviously a popular spot for collectors, as paper trash and empty tin cans were strewn about in untidy fashion. I stood perfectly still, surveying the entire area. To one side was a low concrete wall, probably built to divert the flow at high water. I blinked a couple of times to be sure my eyes were not playing tricks on me. Stretched out motionless against the wall was by far the largest twin-spotted rattlesnake I had ever seen. What luck! I walked slowly over to it, at the same time reaching down to my side for a sack. One sack was already occupied and, to my dismay, I found that a hole had been ripped in the other, probably by one of the yuccas on the slope where I had been diverted by the terrain.

Removing my canteen from its cover, I slowly poured its contents out onto the ground. The snake had still not moved. Gently I reached down and picked up the snake. What a prize! (This snake would eventually be sent, along with a later ridge-nosed, to Carl Kauffeld at the Staten Island Zoo.)

I lowered the snake, tail first, into my canteen and replaced the cap. The snake would have plenty of air to last for several hours and to be sure that it would not become overheated I dipped the canteen into the stream until the canvas cover was soaked. The clouds were moving again as I worked my way back downstream.

As stated before, above the box was a dense stand of New Mexico locust, their oval leaves and thorny branches forming a canopy over the stream. There, suspended amongst the foliage, was the deserted nest of a small bird. Fragments of shell betold a successful hatching. Had the young ones flown the nest or had they the misfortune to be discovered by a green rat snake? I paused, removing the camera strap from around my neck, I leaned over to get a drink from the stream. Suddenly there came a rustling sound from the far side of the stream, not five feet from where I was drinking.

Looking up I found myself face to face with a large green snake—a green rat snake! It had a slender yet muscular body, somewhat larger than my thumb and a good five feet long. The smooth, olive face was reminiscent of the green mamba, a totally unrelated poisonous snake of Africa.

I fumbled for my camera, but before I could bring it into position and remove the cover the snake had disappeared among the tangle of locust. I had taken off my camera and dropped my guard only for a moment, but it had cost me a once-in-a-lifetime picture.

I hurried now, for clouds were moving in faster than anticipated. I entered the box. The channel narrowed, canyon walls closing in on both sides. During high water this section is virtually impassable. I thought to myself, "If only the stream could talk, what stories it would tell—stories of pioneers, conquistadors, miners and gunfighters."

It started to sprinkle. A mule deer, getting a drink from the stream, bolted at my approach, then paused for a second before vanishing into the underbrush.

Later that night Nell told us a strange story that had taken place when she and Bill first moved to the canyon. It was June 12, slightly after midnight, when they were awakened by the sound of riders. Bill, thinking he had forgotten to close the gate, got up to investigate. He stepped outside in time to see three horses, their riders having a lively conversation as they passed. Following on foot, he was suddenly jolted backwards; his way blocked by several strands of wire fence at the forest line. The horses and their riders continued on out of sight.

The next morning when he went down to the gate, he noticed an odd thing. Even though the gate was chained and locked, the hoofprints left by the horses passed right through it. "What's more," Nell continued, "They've been back every year since then. Folks around here say that they're the ghosts of three outlaws who were hanged from a big ol' tree, right here in the canyon."

The following morning we reluctantly said good-bye to the Browns. As we maneuvered the little jeep over the rough road, we had no way of knowing this was the last time we would see Bill. He died of a heart attack during a blizzard that winter while trying to put snow chains on his car.

Nell moved out of the canyon, which is, at this writing, owned and managed by the Nature Conservancy. Reservations are now required in advance for guided tours into the canyon.

John R."Woody" Woodworth, Hamburg Mine, Cochise County, Arizona.

Arizona ridge-nosed rattlesnake

Veronica Williamson with an Arizona (Sonoran) coral snake.

DESERT DENIZENS

The college edition of Webster's New World Dictionary defines *desert* as "an uninhabitable, uncultivated region; wilderness," or "a dry, lifeless region, largely treeless and sandy." Both these definitions are inadequate. The definition most often seen in textbooks on the subject is "a region with less than ten inches annual rainfall." This statement is, of course, both accurate and correct. It does not, however, paint a very vivid picture.

Most people, when they think of deserts, conjure up visions of barren sand dunes, stretching for mile after endless mile, where rattlesnakes and scorpions lurk beneath thorny cacti, and where the bleached bones of hapless animals (or perhaps a stray prospector or two) are scattered across the desolate landscape.

This image, while admittedly romantic, may also be misleading, for deserts are dynamic ecosystems, even the bleakest of which teems with life; one need only take the trouble to look for it.

Beyond Gate's Pass, on the western edge of Tucson, Arizona, lies some of the hottest, driest, most inhospitable country to be found anywhere on the North American continent—the Sonoran Desert, or "Gran Disierto" as it is known in Mexico.

It is to this region that Mabel and I came after our memorable visit with the Browns in Ramsey Canyon. We had several reasons for making the trip. First, we wanted to pay a visit to the world-famous Arizona-Sonora Desert Museum in Tucson. Secondly, it was my desire to photograph a live Gila monster in the wild. And last, I hoped to find and, if possible, to collect one of the most primitive primitive members of the ophidian community found in the United States: a rosy boa, relative of the giant South American constrictors and one of the only two species of "haenophidian" snakes native to the U. S.

We spent most of our first day in rare delight, browsing leisurely through the multitude of exhibits at the museum. As we left we were treated to one of those spectacular desert sunsets such as one usually sees only on calendars and magazine covers.

As darkness folded around, we drove slowly, keeping our eyes on the road ahead. At the "Y" we took the right fork leading to highway 86—also known to veteran snake hunters as the "Ajo Road." Fortunately for us, most of the late hour traffic went the other way, back to town. Before reaching the highway junction, we encountered a lizard less than a foot long ambling slowly across the roadway. I recognized the chunky form immediately as that of a baby Gila monster; the ONLY poisonous lizard found in the United States. Somewhat smaller and less arboreal than the closely related Mexican beaded lizard (*Heloderma horridum*); Gila monsters carry a fat reserve in their tail—an adaptation for surviving extended periods when food is not readily available. Though heavy-bodied, these otherwise sluggish lizards can be astonishingly agile when aroused.

Surprisingly, these vividly colored orange and black lizards can be extremely difficult to spot in their natural habitat against the pale desert sands. This is one of the classic examples of "cryptic coloration" which is designed to conceal by breaking up the outline of the animal. Gila monsters are reported to spend more than eighty-five percent of their life underground, thereby allowing them to conserve moisture by avoiding the extreme conditions often present on the surface. While largely crepuscular, they appear to be most active during the rainy season when, depending upon conditions of temperature and humidity, they are often abroad day or night. These lizards, relatives of the giant monitors and extinct mosasaurs, feed primarily on the eggs and young of ground nesting birds, small mammals and even carrion. The venom, like that of the rattlesnake is largely protein in composition. Produced by glands in the lower jaw, the venom flows through ducts directly into the lizards mouth. Unlike the rattlesnakes, Gila monsters do not posses hollow fangs. A number of teeth, however, are grooved to facilitate the flow of venom into the wound while biting. Due to excessive collecting for the "pet" trade, it has been necessary to legislate protection for these ancient and fascinating lizards.

Our own particular little monster continued walking towards the opposite side of the roadway. At my approach, however, it spun suddenly around to face me, mouth agape menacingly, and emitted a loud hiss; simultaneously licking the air nervously with its broad, forked tongue. This maneuver, calculated to discourage even the most determined predator, caught me by complete surprise, so violent and sudden was this display of temper.

We left him and having reached the main highway, turned west towards Sells. A great horned owl appeared in the beam of our headlights. It had evidently been feeding on the carcass of a dead rabbit. Owls and other predators soon learn about highways, where an easy living is to be made feeding on a plentiful supply of road-kills, such as rabbits and kangaroo rats. Unfortunately from the predators' point of view, however, they often end up as casualties themselves.

Our first snake of the night was a young diamondback. I scooted it off the road and continued driving. A few miles farther along we spotted a second snake. Close inspection revealed this to be a dead long-nosed snake, a victim of modern transportation. The pattern closely resembled that of the California kingsnake, being totally devoid of the red coloration so prominently displayed in the patterns of the eastern subspecies.

We drove on. Another snake. This one was wriggling! It was also a long-nosed snake, an adult female. As I picked it up I discovered blood on my hand. "Another traffic fatality," I cringed. This was happily not the case. In fact, this snake wasn't injured at all, nor had it even been hit. Then I recalled how this particular species typically emits blood from the cloaca when captured or restrained. With a sigh of relief I placed it in one of our unoccupied collecting sacks and handed it to Mabel. This snake later provided the inspiration for a publication titled, "Excavation Behavior in Captive Snakes."

The next snake was a rattler. Although my first thought was another diamondback, it was unmistakably a Mojave, over three feet long and very irritated at our presence. The venom of this species is reportedly, drop by drop, the deadliest of any snake found in the United States. The unique properties of the venom, coupled with an efficient mechanism for injection characteristic of all vipers, make this snake unquestionably our most formidable reptile species. Compounding the danger is its close resemblance to the western diamondback with which it shares a large portion of its range. Both forms have the typical diamond pattern and characteristic black and white banded tail.

There are several ways to tell the two species apart. One is temperament. If it is aggressive, it is probably a diamondback. If it is *more* aggressive, its a Mojave. Of course, a much more scientific way to tell the two species apart is to count the scales on top of the head between the eyes. In the Mojave species there are only two; in the diamondback, four or more. Naturally, these scales are small, and in order to see them you must be very close. I do not recommend this procedure unless one has a great deal of familiarity with rattlesnakes.

Incidentally, the only snake in my entire life that I have had actually pursue me was a small Mojave in Sonora, Mexico. I was standing between it and the only patch of shade for a quarter of a mile, to which this misanthropic Mojave had evidently staked its claim. As I was attempting to photograph it, the snake struck with such vehemence as to actually propel its body forwards. It persisted in this display of dauntless determination until it had, by passing directly between my legs, achieved its purpose. Once in the shade, and after having formed itself into a comfortable coil, it flicked its tongue disdainfully in my direction as if to say, "You may go now."

Among the many strange denizens of the desert is the giant hairy scorpion, one of which now appeared on the roadway. While grotesque in appearance, it is not considered to be among the more dangerous varieties.

A small luminescent figure scampered across the road just ahead. At first I thought it might be yet another scorpion, albeit a smaller version—perhaps even the dreaded *Centuroides*. But it turned out to be one of the most appealing creatures that dwell in the desert, a banded gecko. My initial confusion as to the true identity of the creature was understandable due to its habit of carrying its tail curled forward over its back when walking. These translucent little lizards are often seen wandering about blacktop highways at night after a summer thundershower. Only three inches long including the tail, their most remarkable feature is their voice—an audible, high-pitched squeak reminiscent of the bark of a small dog. This characteristic is unique to the family Gekkonidae. As with the alligator lizards, the tail is disposable.

A strange apparition now appeared in the glow of our headlights. It was our old friend, the Colorado River toad, walking dog-fashion across the highway. It was an odd sight to see one of these huge toads walking in such an ungainly manner. It must have been an especially good area, for these profuse toads were suddenly everywhere, until it seemed impossible to drive without running over them. Perhaps this activity was in anticipation of the deluge which, experience told me, was about to descend upon us with a vengeance.

Another snake! A second Mojave. I dutifully logged him into my field notes: time, 9:30 p.m.; odometer, 93771.0. I tried to show him off the road but he stood his ground, striking furiously. In the process I nearly stepped on a third Mojave lying just outside the headlight beam along the shoulder of the road!

Lightening flashed in the distance. Then again, closer this time. We could hear the thunder. A large snake crawled up onto the roadway. I judged it to be at least five feet long, occupying nearly the entire lane and requiring immediate action. I jammed on the brakes and swerved hard, narrowly missing. Groping for my flashlight, I leapt from the jeep. My eyes were not playing tricks, it really was a kingsnake. I picked up the snake and held it admiringly. Quite possibly an integrade between two subspecies, the Yuma king and the Sonora king. The shiny black and yellow scales shown in the headlights. What a beauty!

Then, with a crash that shook the jeep, it was as if a giant hand had reached out and unzipped the clouds. The rain poured down over the sheetmetal cab as the vacuum wipers tried frantically to keep up. "Not a very good place to be if there is a flash flood," I said. Suddenly our way was blocked by a torrent of water. There was nothing to do now but wait. Over the next hour or so two more vehicles arrived. At least we had company.

It was 3:00 a.m. when the water finally subsided enough to get through. We picked our way carefully between boulders that had been washed down by floodwaters. The other vehicles followed close behind.

We made it! Now it was on to Organ Pipe and a cozy motel room for the night. Luck was with us, however; just outside the monument we picked up a small saddled leaf-nosed snake, likewise a victim of modern transportation. This handsome snake had wide chocolate bands against a pinkish-tan background. It had crawled up onto the elevated roadway to escape the floods, only to meet with what to me seemed like a no less ignominious end. With a tinge of sadness, I dropped the lifeless little snake into one of our preserving jars.

The sky was clear the following morning. Desert gravel doesn't hold water for long, and the casual observer probably wouldn't notice that the stems of the ocotillo had swollen, taking fullest advantage of whatever water may have reached their roots. The stately and picturesque saguaros had undoubtedly received their share of the life-giving water as well. Without these summer thunderstorms most of the plants and animals that live in the desert would perish.

We left our car in the main campground and hiked along one of the narrow trails that meander through the monument. The two reptile species in greatest evidence were the western whiptail lizard and the desert iguana. Both of these wary lizards provide the nature photographer with hours of challenging entertainment. After nearly an hour of entertainment and no pictures, however, it was time to put my contingency plan into action.

Removing from my field bag a telescoping rod (courtesy of an old radio antenna), I carefully fashioned a loop of nylon fish line at its tip. I then drove as closer to one of the desert iguanas as possible without sending it into full retreat. The lizards did not seem to take alarm as quickly when approached by auto.

The plan worked. After several unsuccessful attempts, I finally managed to secure the noose about the lizard's neck and one shoulder. Allowing it to put one foot through the noose not only prevents the lizard from backing out at the critical moment, it also reduces the likelihood of injury. With a little handling I was able to pose the lizard and get a suitable picture.

The desert iguana is a remarkable animal, a classic example of how organism specialize for life in an extreme environment. A number of intriguing studies have been done on the physiology of this particular species, studies which may help shed some light on the mysteries of man's own physiological mechanisms.

Mathew Kluger was able to induce a fever response in these lizards by injecting them with a bacteria *Aeromonas hydrophila*. He thereby demonstrated the role of fever in combating infectious disease, and ended a medical controversy that began over twenty-four hundred years ago. This study is remarkable in that it was conducted on a "cold-blooded" animal. In fact, the subject was deliberately chosen for its ability to exert behavioral control over its preferred body temperature.

The desert iguana is remarkable in other respects as well. Free water is seldom available in the lizard's natural habitat. In addition, many of the plants upon which the species depends for food contain high concentrations of salt. This means the iguanas must devise some ingenious mechanisms for maintaining a proper electrolyte balance under conditions of severe water deprivation. Like many desert reptiles, *Dipsosaurus* is able to satisfy some of its moisture requirements by absorbing water directly through its skin. However, this is a two way street, which may help to explain why they spend so much of the day in their burrows where the water vapor pressure is much higher than it is above ground. Another interesting phenomenon is their ability to excrete salt through special glands associated with the nares. This salt can sometimes be seen in the form of a white crust around each nostril.

A common problem among desert reptiles, including iguanas, is the elimination of ammonia, a natural by-product of metabolism, while at the same time conserving vital body fluids. Many reptiles, desert and non-desert alike, solve this problem by converting ammonia into insoluble uric acid which, when dried, becomes a yellowish-white chalky substance. This analogy is a good one, for it makes a suitable substitute should one suddenly find himself out of chalk. What marvelous ingenuity we find in nature!

The Ajo Road is legendary. Numerous pages have been filled with accounts of unexcelled "cruising" along this remote stretch of blacktop highway—bags filled to overflowing with all manner of snakes, not to mention an assorted variety of other creepy-crawlies, along with, of course, the usual allusions to "banana-peel lizards" and "fan-belt snakes." Night after night and mile after mile, the stories are the same until they blend into one another, forming anonymous impressions of snakes in seemingly endless supply and variety. These stories are substantially true.

One of the most memorable nights on the Sonoran Desert was spent cruising the Buckeye Road. In one thirty-five mile stretch from Gila Bend to Buckeye, I encountered no less than seven different reptile species, one of which I had never collected before—the beautiful and delicate shovel-nosed snake.

We left Gila Bend at 10:00 p.m.; the temperature was a cool ninety-five degrees. We continued north along the old Buckeye Road, a stretch of highway that parallels the Gila River and which, on this occasion, proved unusually productive. The first snake was the prize of the evening, an adult shovel-nosed snake, fully eight inches long and beautifully marked with a truly spectacular pattern of alternating chocolate-brown and orange bars on a cream background.

Another welcome addition to my collection was a pair of young sidewinders we picked up south of Gillespie Dam. Now, regardless of how one happens to be predisposed toward snakes, sidewinders are "cute"—a small rattlesnake with a round face and a projection of the supraocular scale over each eye resembling a horn, hence the popular epithet "horned rattler." The term "sidewinder" derives from this snake's peculiar mode of progression, a distinction shared with an unrelated species of Old World viper which is similar in appearance and occupies a similar ecological niche. Its progression is best described by analogy to a coiled spring rolling along on its side. Although somewhat irregular, this odd behavior bestows upon the snake certain advantages, not the least of which is its thermoregulatory function. If you have ever walked barefoot on a hot sidewalk, you can easily appreciate that, as the snake crawls, a portion of its undersurface is raised above the hot sand at any given time. This allows for the passage of air between the snake's belly and the ground, thereby contributing to his sense of comfort. This peculiarity also affords another advantage; increased traction on the shifting desert sands.

Another remarkable feature of these little rattlesnakes is there almost total independence from free water; they derive all of the moisture they require from their food which consists primarily of lizards and an occasional small rodent. I have kept a sidewinder alive for years without ever offering it fresh water. On other occasions I have witnessed sidewinders which, although refusing to drink from a container, would lap droplets of water trapped between the keels of their scales, this following an infrequent cage sprinkling with tepid water. I suspect this is not an uncommon occurrence in nature.

In spite of its bad reputation in cowboy movies, the much-maligned sidewinder is hardly capable of inflicting a lethal bite on a healthy adult human receiving even minimal first aid care.

As we have seen, a number of reptiles employ sophisticated physiological and behavioral means to maintain an internal homeothermic environment optimal for metabolic efficiency. Therefore, any discussion of temperature regulation in reptiles brings to mind several interesting questions. Foremost among them: are reptiles really "cold blooded?" In attempting to answer this question, scientists have had to rely on innovation and intuition. Dr. Charles M. Bogert, Curator Emeritus of the American Museum of Natural History, stated that "the interaction of structure and behavior makes it difficult to design experiments testing one or another of the reptile's temperature regulating attributes."

Subsequent investigations involving both recent and prehistoric forms have necessitated a change in thinking about cold-bloodedness in reptiles. In reviewing paleontological material, the line between "warm-blooded" and "cold-blooded" becomes a fine line indeed. When, for example did the first birds, pterosaurs and the therapsid ancestors of mammals, first achieve their warm-blooded status? In all cases this was most certainly a gradual process and was not the exclusive invention of any one group. Reptiles, in fact, have demonstrated remarkable plasticity in this regard. And, as witnessed by the myriad of insect-eating lizards which compete successfully with their insectivorous mammalian counterparts, warm-bloodedness may not always be an advantage. Dr. James A. Peters, of the United States National Museum and author of the Dictionary of Herpetology, addresses the matter definitively:

> COLD BLOODED, n. = ECTOTHERM. Although often used in herpetological literature, this term is singularly inappropriate, since the temperature of many reptiles may often be well above that of "warm bloods" in the same environment.

In the summer of 1985 we'd just been to visit Nell who was now staying with her daughter in Tucson. As night fell, we decided to go for a short drive on the west side. It had been nearly an hour since we'd seen any pavement. We'd crossed a wide valley and were now proceeding towards some rocky hills. We were in unfamiliar territory. The ground was damp but there was no standing water. There was lightening in the distance. I'd scooted a Gila monster off the "road" bout half an hour earlier and although the air was warm and relatively humid, we hadn't seen any other activity since then; not so much as a scorpion. Still, I felt a sense of anticipation.

The girls were dozing off in the back seat. I looked over at Mabel. She was looking straight ahead. I squinted and stared out at the edge of the high beams. We drove slowly, about twenty miles an hour. Then there was the looping form of a snake in the headlights. I stopped. I jumped out with a pillow case in one hand and my hook in the other. Frozen in the headlights really was – a tiger—rattlesnake, a young one; and not at all happy to see me.

It made a sudden dive for the side of the road as I moved to block its path. Reaching out with my hook, I attempted to draw him back but he slid gracefully off the hook. He reminded me of some of the mountain rattlesnakes I had encountered. He made a beeline for the rocks. I only had one chance. Once again, with my hook, I guided him towards a small bush, hoping to boost his confidence. It worked. Backing up to the bush he rattled vigorously and moved his head back and forth. I managed to pin his head and gently lifted him, writhing, into the pillow case then twisted it quickly so that he wouldn't come shooting back out again. I took a breath and looked around. By now the entire family was out of the car, positioning themselves in a semicircle around me. My very first live tiger.

I was entirely lost. The road was pretty good. That gave me confidence. I saw bright lights far off in the distance. It was probably an industrial facility of some sort.

We drove for another hour and then, finally, pulled up to a blacktop road. There was some sort of store but at this hour all the lights were out. We followed the pavement for a while and finally came to a freeway exit. Now we pointed the car towards Tucson.

Back in Tucson, Mabel headed for bed, while the girls decided to take a dip in the motel pool. I opted to sit in a lawn chair and relax. As the lightening approached, I suggested we should all turn in and try to get some sleep for what was left of the night.

In the morning I was, of course, anxious to get pictures of our new found treasure. We headed back towards the "scene of the crime," as it were. We pulled in front of the little store we'd checked out the night before and went inside. I tried my best to explain where I thought we had been the previous evening.

"Nope," replied the owner, leaning his elbows on the counter. "You can't get here from there. The bridge is out."

I hadn't crossed any bridge, I thought to myself. I took the scenic route.

Tiger rattlesnake

Gila monster

CLOSE ENCOUNTERS

During the course of my herpetological career, I have frequently been called upon to present programs on the subject to various groups. These programs have been primarily of an educational nature, but I have tried to make them entertaining as well. This, I might add, has usually been an enjoyable and rewarding experience for me; the outcome, however, is not always what one has anticipated.

Keeping this in mind, I now offer the following anecdote which I have—somewhat reluctantly—resurrected from my "For What Its Worth" file. I might also take this opportunity to remind the reader that, in most instances when a person is injured by an animal, the animal is acting in self-defense.

Now, Gila monsters (as we all know) hail from an ancient and honorable lineage. There is, however, a dark side to their nature, for these marvelous creatures are endowed with rows of sharp teeth which are grooved to accommodate the flow of their venom—produced by glands in the lower jaw—and not (as used to be believed) as a consequence of any alleged deficiency in their digestive tract. The venom itself contains a component which appears to serve no other useful purpose than to produce the excruciating pain often associated with their bite (which can be fatal).

The following event occurred during the final semester of my senior year at college. I had been asked to give a program on reptiles to a group of high school students. To help illustrate my talk I brought with me several live reptiles, including one very handsome nineteen-inch Gila monster. As the result of a momentary distraction, the Gila monster managed to secure a good grip on the index finger of my right hand. As hand and lizard were simultaneously withdrawn from the muslin sack in which the lizard had been transported, the lizard retained its grip with bulldog tenacity.

The school teacher stood there dumbfounded. In fact, of the seventy or so students in the room at the time, only three or four seemed to be aware that anything out of the ordinary had transpired.

Meanwhile, the offending reptile was chewing his way along my finger in much the same way as you or I might eat an ear of corn. One tooth had actually penetrated my fingernail.

I looked around for something that could be used as a wedge, and spied the lid to a slide projector. With this I gently pried at the little monster's mouth. I was worried that too much pressure might fracture his jaw.

Crack! The little blighter had chewed his way through the lid and, with a somewhat detached gaze, now continued his steady progression towards the proximal end of my finger and ultimately, I surmised, to my elbow. Still he showed no inclination to relinquish his viselike hold. A different plan of action was clearly indicated.

Again I searched for an appropriate implement. Retaining my calm and collected demeanor as best I could under the circumstances, and with the assistance of a wooden chair (which I managed by guile and cunning to substitute for my finger), I was able to free myself from the jaws of this miniature Tyrannosaur!

To my great relief, the lizard was uninjured. I replaced him in the bag. After tying the bag securely, I handed it to the teacher—who addressed it with all the enthusiasm with which I envision a proper lady would handle a night crawler.

I remembered to walk, not run (one never runs under these circumstances as it only hastens the spread of venom into the system), down the stairs, across the street and into the biology building—luckily I had been giving this lecture on the U.N.M. campus.

Standing in the doorway to Dr. Degenhardt's office, blood streaming from my finger, I felt pale. As he looked up from his desk, I said "I've been bitten by a Gila monster."

Shortly I was lying on a stretcher and my hand was placed in a plastic bag inside a gallon jar filled with Ice cubes and water. While one person called the hospital emergency room, five more carried me to Bill's Waiting Land Rover.

At the hospital my hand was removed from the ice water and placed in a basin of hot, soapy water. Up until then I had only thought I felt pain!

John Applegarth and Ted Brown, after supplying the attending physicians an extensive bibliography on Gila monster bites, were finally able to locate my wife and relate to her the events of the morning.

Now Gila monster venom appears to work differently on different people, depending on circumstances. The slug of codeine, with which I had been injected, did its job and I was becoming less coherent by the minute—not so much so that I couldn't feel the pain, however.

The doctor was now reading aloud: "The use of opiates in the treatment of Gila monster bites is contra-indicated..." Now they tell me. I looked at my hand—all the color had gone out of it. It was as white as the bed sheet.

"We may have to remove those fingers," one doctor mused, examining my hand intently through his bi-focals. "No circulation in there at all."

Another doctor entered the room and announced optimistically, "Dr. Stahnky over in Arizona has some antivenin that he has developed specifically for Gila monsters. Of course," he went on, "...it's never been tried on humans before."

Pressure was mounting. Now I remembered that I had a bacteriology lab final day after tomorrow. I couldn't miss that.

At the last minute my fingers got a reprieve. Actually, the credit goes to a passing gynecologist—to whom I shall be forever grateful. It seems that the venom had excited nerves, causing constriction of the arteries, thereby cutting off circulation to the hand. He could give me a nerve block, the doctor explained, similar to the saddle block given to women in labor.

Why not? It was certainly worth a try!

He returned momentarily with his kit and unwrapped all of the necessary paraphernalia. In spite of his friendly smile and pleasant manner, to approach a patient in pain with a needle of that magnitude necessitated an extremely refined approach. "I'm going to stick this needle in your armpit," he said, "and I want you to tell me when I hit the nerve." On only the eighth try he hit the spot and it wasn't really necessary for me to tell him.

It worked! I watched with some relief as the color returned to my hand. Of course, now my forearm was completely numb. No matter how it was moved, as far as my arm was concerned, it was always in the same position as it had been at the time of the injection. This side effect, I was assured, was only temporary.

The following morning I got up, dressed and walked over to the campus. After finishing my bacteriology test, I returned to my hospital bed—just in time for the nurse to come in and take her daily blood samples. My blood was of special interest, she explained, as the doctors intended to publish my case history and it was therefore necessary to do extensive analyses. But seven vials, in my opinion, should have been enough to do a whole transfusion!

The following day, after receiving my farewell penicillin injection, I was released from the hospital. As I turned to leave, Dr. Heffrin told me, "Be sure to sign out, you were half way across Lomas yesterday before we realized you were gone."

"I had to take a lab' final in bacteriology," I protested.

Another incident worth repeating I like to call the "Mysterious Box" episode.

From the fall of 1969 until spring of the following year, I had been doing taxonomic work on specimens shipped to me from Lee Anderson—who had, by some nefarious scheme, managed to have himself assigned to the 20th Preventative Medical Unit at Bien Hua, Vietnam.

Each specimen had attached to it a plastic identification number. I simply verified the I.D.'s and reported any discrepancies back to the Unit. In the process I managed to accumulate a sizeable collection of Southeast Asian "herps", which were eventually deposited in the Museum of Southwestern Biology at U.N.M., pursuant to Lee's request.

These preserved specimens were all properly tagged and labeled so there could not possibly be any confusion as to which identification belonged to which snake or lizard. The project also gave me a chance to keep up with Lee's activities, and so I was glad to do it (not to mention the valuable knowledge I was gaining about the herpetofauna of Southeast Asia).

In March of 1970, an unseasonable storm had forced me to cut short a trip to the Animas Mountains. I returned home in the early morning hours of the 30th, thoroughly exhausted. I had been sustaining myself for the last three hundred miles on a thermos of black coffee. Rubbing my eyes and dragging my gear behind me, I entered the front room. In the middle of the floor stood a large metal box. Upon the box were many unmistakable symbols indicating the deadly and poisonous nature of its contents.

Regrouping what little was left of my senses, I approached the box and, after loosening a series of straps and latches, soon had the container open, to reveal a variety of bags of assorted sizes, colors and dimensions. I was ecstatic. While I'd received shipments from other parts of the world (Africa and South America), this was my first shipment of live reptiles from Asia.

I lifted the largest bag. The unmistakable coils of a large snake could be easily discerned through the canvas, even in my somewhat bewildered condition. A python! I was sure of it. Quickly I released the tie string. Reaching into the bag, I scooped up the snake and held it admiringly before me. It was slender and black, about six feet long, with smooth, shiny scales. It was also not a python. As if to underscore this point, the snake turned to face me, raised its head and, slowly spreading its hood, emitted a short, sinister hiss! I stood like a stone statue, not daring to move. There is, you see, no specific antivenin for the bite of the Southeast Asian cobra.

There were six or seven other people in the room at the time, including my wife, so it was necessary to suppress my first inclination: throw the snake and run. I inched slowly towards my open grub box. As my hand hovered over the box, I withdrew it suddenly, dropping in the snake, and quickly closed the lid with my other hand.

I again turned my attention to the shipping container. It was now that I noticed the cloth I.D. tags securely fastened to each sack. They did, in fact, contain several pythons—as well as cobras, pit vipers and a variety of other snakes and lizards. It was not until I had removed the last bag from the container, however, that I discovered the tag for the cobra.

An interesting episode involving this particular cobra deserves mention. It was related to me some time after Lee's return from his tour of duty in Vietnam. He was going through some of his army memorabilia, among which I noted a Bronze Star and pressed him for details.

Lee somewhat hesitantly acknowledged that it was awarded for an incident in Bien Hua when he was asked to crawl under a woodpile outside the mess tent to retrieve this very snake. The only accessible portion of the snake was its tail, and some maneuvering on Lee's part was necessary to retrieve it.

Lee was never a show-off and I subsequently hesitated to mention the incident as it seemed to embarrass him. I doubt, however, that this was a sentiment shared by a division of hungry G.I.s. And, as I mentioned before, there is no antivenin for the venom of this particular variety of cobra. This was an act which required a clear head and a degree of confidence acquired by considerable experience in handling poisonous snakes—not bravado!

Shortly after the "Mysterious Box" episode, it was either late fall or early spring, I can't be certain, having been bitten by the Varanus bug. . . . *Varanus*, that genus of lizards which includes such friendly forms as the Komodo dragon and the crocodile monitor, you know, the monitor lizards. Fascinating creatures to be sure. I had decided to contact Richard Leakey, the son of anthropological icons Mary and Lewis Leakey, about the possibility of sending me a few adult Nile monitors. I arranged to have some money deposited in a bank in Kenya, to cover expenses, and he agreed to make the shipment as soon as he could "round them up."

Now, I should tell you that Nile monitors are not to be taken lightly. They attain a length of 5' or 6', have long curved teeth with which they can demolish a credit card (as I found out the hard way) and razor sharp claws. They are not to be trifled with.

On the morning of the package's arrival I received a message from the freight office at the Albuquerque International Airport. When I arrived, there were three black sedans parked at the loading dock. One of them was Department of Agriculture, another was U. S. Customs and a third that had no insignia what-so-ever. I remember feeling like I must be an important person to garner all this attention. As I stepped inside the door I observed a wooden crate, three ft. by three ft. by six inches, setting on the counter. The freight attendant handed me a large screwdriver and everyone stood around watching while I pried open the box.

As I lifted the lid I could see six large lizards with their tails folded next to their bodies and each stuffed into its own lady's nylon stocking like so many sausages! What I discovered next was very sad indeed. They were frozen "solid."

The box had gone first from Kenya to France where it was put on a plane bound for Chicago. Chicago was socked in by a blizzard so the plane had to be diverted to Ontario, where the blizzard was headed next. In Ontario the box sat on a loading dock over night, arriving at the Albuquerque International Airport the following day. This was quite a shock to me. As you can imagine, I was gravely disappointed.

I picked up one of the lizards and tapped it gently against the counter. Thump, thump. The man from agriculture reached in and picked up some of the shredded packing material and rubbed some of the fibers between his fingers. The customs inspector then leaned over to take a good look. Everything seemed to be in order, except for the lizards. As I headed out the door the freight attendant asked if I'd mind taking the crate and its contents to the dumpster. "Sure," I said dejectedly. I picked up the crate and carried it to my car.

When I got home I carried the lizards into the bathroom where I filled the tub with tap water from the "cold" faucet. Removing the lizards from their sleeves I gently placed them, one by one, in the tub. After about ten minutes I began to notice some twitching, then an eye opening, ever so slightly. After about twenty minutes I had a bathroom full of four to five foot lizards all scrambling to get out. Who'd have thought?

BIG BEND

In the rugged Big Bend country of southwest Texas, the Rio Grande flows steadily southeastward towards the Gulf of Mexico, then veers suddenly to the north, creating one of our most familiar national landmarks. Here, in the oases formed by run-off from the Chisos Mountains lives a unique little pit viper, the trans-Pecos copperhead. In the spring of 1979 I was determined to find and photograph this rare subspecies in its native habitat. In addition to my family, I was accompanied by my old friend Ted Brown, his charming wife Sue and a young reptile enthusiast, Doug Duerre. Actually, Doug was more interested in lizards than snakes, and what he lacked in age and experience was more than adequately compensated for by his enthusiasm. But now to my story.

As the sun rose over Castolon Peak the desert below was serene and peaceful. The plaintive wail of a mourning dove drifted across the desolate landscape. A black-tailed jackrabbit loped from one clump of mesquite to the next, pausing for a moment to listen, then moving on, keeping an ever-wary eye out for predators.

Mabel heated up the coffee and put the bacon on to fry while Doug and I put away our bedrolls and made preparations for the day's hunt. "Its going to be a hot one today," he predicted, gazing up into the pale blue sky. We hurried through breakfast and loaded our gear into the Scout (which by now had replaced the old family jeep).

It was nine o'clock when we arrived in Panther Junction. Our friends, Ted and Sue Brown, were there waiting for us. We spent the next half-hour talking with the rangers at Park Headquarters, gathering as much information as possible about road conditions, weather forecasts and scheduled programs.

We then started north along highway 385 towards "Dagger Flats." About fifteen miles from the junction, Ted, who was in the lead, waved us to a halt. This was one of the sites where Bill Degenhardt had done population studies on whiptail lizards as part of his doctoral dissertation. Ted had spent nearly an entire summer with Bill in the park and wanted to see what changes had taken place in the ten years or so since he last visited the spot.

He was able to locate a couple of re-bar posts used to define the boundaries of the plot. We took a few photographs for posterity and then continued on up the Avery Canyon road towards "Dagger Flats" (so-named for the giant dagger yuccas, a unique and conspicuous element of the local flora).

Off to our right was the "fossil bone exhibit." As I read the sign I was reminded that it was here in Big Bend where *Quetzalcoatlus*, "the largest creature ever to fly," had been discovered by a student working in the extensive Mesozoic fossil beds of the region. Paleontologists had surmised that this giant pterosaur was the reptile equivalent of a vulture, a scavenger feeding primarily on carrion—perhaps even the carcasses of dead dinosaurs.

Leaving the highway at this point, we wound our way up a short dirt road terminating at a bluff, across from which was a small shelter, built by park staff to protect the fossilized skull and jawbone of an extinct ungulate, "in situ" as it were. On our way up the path to the shelter our youngest daughter, Carmen, spotted a Texas horned toad and was soon in hot pursuit. She returned shortly and I could tell by her wide smile she had been successful. Her brown eyes sparkled with pride as she opened two stubby hands to reveal a spiny-looking lizard (the "horned toad" is actually a lizard, related to the iguanas of all things, and not a toad at all). This one was about three inches long.

Veronica, Carmen's sister and fourteen months her senior, and who was unusually reserved for a seven year old, insisted on knowing why it was so flat. "That has to do with `thermoregulation'," I explained. This elicited a frown from the younger. I went on to explain that these lizards and, in fact, all reptiles living under the harsh conditions imposed on desert dwellers, must maintain their body temperatures within tolerable limits, or they will die. On cool mornings the "horned toad" flattens himself out on the sand to take full advantage of the sun's warmth. Later on, should he become too warm, he simply tilts sideways so that the greater area of his surface is not exposed to the sun. In this position he can actually cool himself by radiating heat from his shaded surfaces.

The girls listened politely. "Anyway, I went on to explain, "we cant keep him, its against park rules." Reluctantly, Carmen lowered the lizard to the rocky ground, stroking it affectionately behind the head as one might do to a puppy.

Meanwhile, Veronica had discovered a bat beneath the eaves of the shelter and was gently encouraging it with the stalk of a long-deceased yucca. Bats are plentiful in the park, but this one looked sick. "Don't touch it," I cautioned, recalling that on an earlier visit Ted had been bitten by a bat and, rather than make the long drive each day to the nearest doctor's office, had given *himself* the rabies series (bats have been known to transmit the disease)—a rather unpleasant experience. When Ted tells the story he is quick to add, with modesty, that a steady diet of sardines and jalapeno relish had dulled his senses, making the pain bearable.

Returning to our vehicle I caught a glimpse of red and green, soon revealed to be the head and shoulders of a greater earless lizard. Camera in hand, I managed to work my way close enough for a picture before he made good his escape.

By now it was too late to catch up with Ted and Sue. We would meet them at the "old ranch" which, as had been determined by prior arrangement, would be our midday rendezvous point.

A collared lizard scampered across the road as we passed—running on its hind legs, tail curled over its back—I was reminded of a miniature archosaurian from the "age of reptiles."

The sun was directly overhead when we arrived. A metal bar across the entrance prevented access by vehicle, but it was only a short walk to the now crumbling adobe structure that had once been the ranch house.

The old windmill, long since abandoned, squeaked incessantly, a reminder of bygone days when caring hands greased its bearings and replaced its worn-out parts. Then it stopped. A breeze no longer afforded relief from the oppressive heat. A family of javelina grunted nervously from the shade of a creosote bush. Even the cicadas, those raucous little insects so often heard but seldom seen, were conspicuous by their silence. Curiously, I hadn't really noticed them before. The cicadas were a good sign, for I had heard that it's during the cicada bloom that copperheads are most active.

The ancient fig trees provided welcome shade and we refreshed ourselves in a small basin of crystal water beneath the windmill. Ted and Sue arrived with the "grub" and as we ate, the temperature soared above the one-hundred-degree mark.

The afternoon passed quickly and nightfall found Doug and me cruising slowly along the blacktop highway in search of "creepy-crawlies." We weren't having much luck—"too much moon and too little moisture"—a statement reflecting traditional snake-hunting beliefs as much as scientific fact. We saw a dead western diamondback rattlesnake which had been run over not long before we arrived. Doug made the appropriate notation in the log—"D.O.R.," signifying that the animal had, in fact, been found *dead on the road.* Two more hours of road cruising turned up nothing. It was 2:00 a.m. when we arrived back at our camp near Castolon.

I was up before dawn. Sunrise on the desert is an experience you don't want to miss; like sunsets and snowflakes, no two are alike. Doug and the girls collected firewood, while I loaded a fresh roll of film onto the camera and gathered our equipment together. A quick cup of coffee and we were all set.

Twenty minutes later Doug and I had parked the Scout and were heading up the narrow switchback trail that afforded our only access to Santa Elena Canyon. Here the timeless waters of the Rio Grande, called the "Rio Bravo" in Mexico, have cut deep into the rock, carving out precipitous cliffs which form the canyon walls. We stood there for a moment in wonderment dwarfed by the immensity of the scene.

The trail had been partially obliterated by floodwaters, necessitating a slow and cautious descent into the canyon. The loose sand made walking difficult and thick stands of canegrass could just as easily have concealed a band of peccaries, let alone a snake.

Doug hurried on ahead of me, keeping a sharp eye on the sand for any clues that might indicate the presence of a snake. The sand was already too hot for a snake to be out in the open. Doug paused, then motioned me forward; this could only mean one thing. Kneeling, we examined the track, which appeared to be fresh. The pressure ridges indicated the direction of travel.

The trail led down the steep bank and into a clump of grass, the roots of which were exposed by floodwaters. The sun's glare against the sand made me squint as I tried to make out the shadowy shapes amongst the maze of tangled roots.

There! The vivid coloration was unmistakably that of a juvenile copperhead, about thirty-five centimeters long. Its concealment was enhanced by alternating light and dark bands, breaking up the snake's outline against the pale sand. This was one of the best examples of cryptic coloration I had seen. Slowly I reached up and pried loose the snake from its hiding place. It seemed unperturbed by this treatment and acknowledged our presence only with rapid flicks of its pink tongue. The tongue, of course, is quite harmless. It is associated with the Jacobson's, or vomarine organ, an important sense organ of snakes and some lizards which allows them to gather olfactory information about there surroundings. It is especially important in tracking prey and avoiding predators.

Up until now the little fellow had seemed quiescent. Out on the hot sand, however, it was a different story. As the camera clicked away, the snake began to look around nervously.

Now although snake hunting, whether as a hobby or for serious scientific investigation, provides the enthusiast with a certain amount of diversion, it can be hazardous. Moreover, when photographing poisonous species in the wild, a certain amount of risk is unavoidable, especially when it is necessary to photograph them at close range. As fate would have it, a blade of grass had fallen in front of the camera lens. As I reached out to brush it aside, and without taking my eye from the viewfinder, I came to a sudden realization. I had been using a new lens, one with a different focal length than I was used to, which had caused me to misjudge the distance between me and my subject. A regrettable miscalculation! Warmed by the sun from above and the hot sand from below, this recalcitrant reptile did not hesitate to embed his fangs in the second knuckle of my right index finger. Regaining my composure, I continued to take more pictures as the "offending reptile" hastily made his way back into the safety of his hideout.

Doug had been watching the proceedings with some interest. At my coaxing, he too had been closer to our scaly little friend than prudence would dictate.

"That's just great," I said somewhat disgustedly. I was a little surprised that my finger had started to swell so quickly, considering the size of the snake. Also, copperhead venom is not as toxic as that of rattlesnakes—or so I had been led to believe. Besides, it appeared that one fang puncture was only superficial, barely penetrating the skin. Nevertheless, a small, purplish area was visible at the puncture site. I spit out the blood and venom mixture and continued sucking my now throbbing finger as we made our way back up the trail.

A male Merriam's spiny lizard, hanging head down on the vertical face of his favorite rock, watched with trepidation at our passing. I managed to snap a picture before he retired to the sanctuary of a nearby crevice. As I continued photographing the canyon and its inhabitants, I noticed a progressive stiffness in my now distended finger.

Our return to camp was uneventful. We decided to wait out the afternoon heat and make our supply run into Panther Junction that evening. I crushed some ice in a towel and wrapped it about my swollen hand. Then I laid back in the shade and tried to get some sleep. The stifling heat made sleeping difficult and I finally gave up. We drove into Panther Junction in spite of the heat, which once again was well over the one-hundred-degree mark.

By dusk Doug and I were again on our way back to Santa Elena canyon. It was already getting dark as we crossed over Terlingua Creek, now reduced to a series of shallow pools in anticipation of the summer rains, and began making our way for the second time up the steep trail.

In the dim light I was surprised to see a ground snake lying in full view on the path. This was a small, grayish-colored snake with a smooth, cylindrical body about twenty centimeters long. Its drab coloration was in marked contrast to the often brightly colored individuals with which I was more familiar from New Mexico. Even snakes from the same population demonstrate surprising variation in color and pattern, displaying a bewildering array of orange and black bands and stripes and every conceivable variation thereof. This points to the interesting fact that it is not always possible to identify a snake by its color pattern alone. I attached the flash unit to my camera and took a couple of pictures, working the shutter release button with my middle finger.

We proceeded down into the canyon as before. Doug carried the flashlight, working it back and forth slowly over the sand. I thought I saw an eye shine in the dense stand of cane grass along the river. Doug searched the edge of the cane grass with the light. There, in the dim glow of the flashlight was a brightly banded snake, unmistakably a copperhead, about three feet long.

Doug placed the rubber sole of his boot gently on the snake's tail while I attempted to focus my camera in the failing light. The snake struck, imbedding its fangs in the leather boot top. Then, in a surprising maneuver, it began to crawl up Doug's pant leg! This was too much, even for Doug. He went straight up. I don't know where the snake went.

We continued walking in the soft sand, speaking almost in whispers—why, I'm not sure, since snakes are supposed to be deaf to airborne sounds. Perhaps it was the immensity of the canyon at night, the self awareness of our own almost insignificant presence in this awesome setting.

Another one! A small one, but with the brightest metallic colors we had seen so far, and from which the species takes its popular name. Doug held the flashlight close to the snake while I photographed it.

A little farther up the canyon another copperhead had climbed up into the cane grass in pursuit of a cicada. It dropped to the ground at our approach and disappeared in the underbrush. Doug hesitated.

"Listen," he said in a low tone.

We stood there in the darkness, neither of us moving. As Doug directed his light into the dense grass, we could make out the familiar forms of two snakes, each about two feet long. Possibly a pair!

We continued on, photographing first one snake and then another. By the time we finally made our way back to the mouth of the canyon we had seen eleven copperheads! This, our last night in the park, had truly been a night to remember.

The early morning sun cast long shadows across the desert. I lay there in my bedroll for a few minutes listening to the silence. I looked at my hand. By now the first three fingers were distended and the swelling had progressed part way up my wrist.

We arrived at the basin in time for breakfast. Ted and Sue were expecting us.

"Where were you guys yesterday?' Sue asked.

With a tinge of embarrassment, I held up my hand.

"Oh, I see you've been up in copperhead country," Ted laughed. And then, never being one to pass up an opportunity, he added, "Let me get a picture of that hand." Later, with a hearty meal under our belts, we were prepared for any contingency.

Sue now brought out a pillowcase, tied at the top in a square knot. She opened it to reveal an alligator lizard, about twelve centimeters "snout to vent." She went on to explain that she and Ted had hiked over to Green Gulch the day before where they found the lizard in some leaf litter. Ted had kept it for pictures and was going to take it back and release it.

We went along for the ride. Actually, I'll do almost anything for a picture, especially one of such an unusual animal as this— somewhat larger and less distinctly banded than the related species with which I had become familiar in Arizona. Following an invigorating hike through Green Gulch, we said good-bye to the Browns. We made a brief stop in Panther Junction to fill up our gas tanks in anticipation of the long drive ahead.

A buzzard, carried by a thermal, soared high above us. A "dust-devil" swirled lazily across the desert floor. One lone agave stood sentinel beside the long black ribbon of asphalt highway. "Yes," I thought to myself, "selective pressures have produced many seemingly strange and bizarre creatures here in the desert. But they all share a single purpose: survival." If we hurried we could be in Carlsbad before dark.

Billy Atkins (formerly head reptile-keeper at the Rio Grande Zoo) and I returned to Big Bend in August of that same year. I was curious to see whether the copperheads would be active under a different set of circumstances. May had been hot and dry. We had been there during the full moon and had experienced terrific winds almost every night from midnight until dawn. On this second trip the weather was cloudy, relatively humid, with early evening breezes and almost no moon.

We had just crossed over the state line into Texas and were proceeding south towards Van Horn when we saw a large coachwhip crossing the roadway ahead. We managed to stop the car just in time to avoid hitting the snake, and were soon in pursuit on foot. It moved with deceptive speed and agility for so large a snake, which we estimated to be in excess of six feet. It instinctively took advantage of available cover which, in this case, was provided by a liberal scattering of thorny mesquite. Attempts to follow it through the savage tangles proved to be very difficult. Time and again we thought we had it cut off from escape, only to discover that we had been out-maneuvered. The snake showed no signs of tiring and, upon finding its retreat blocked, would lunge menacingly with wide open mouth. As I soon found out, lacerations from those razor sharp teeth bleed profusely. The snake won out in the end with a little help from a barbed wire fence.

We arrived at the park much later than anticipated, well after dark, and proceeded directly to Santa Elena Canyon.

Another and unexpected eventuality was that Terlingua Creek, instead of being a series of shallow pools, was now a full-blown river which would have to be forded if we were to reach our objective. The silt, washed down by floodwaters, was as treacherous as quicksand. As I waded apprehensively into the churning muddy water, I began to sink—first to my ankles, then to my knees—as the sandy bottom seemed to disintegrate beneath my feet. Darkness was everywhere. It was impossible to see my hand held six inches in front of my face. Bill followed, carrying our only flashlight ("I figured there were two crazy people out there in the river that night," Bill later confided to me.

Suddenly there was a series of sloshing sounds, as if some unseen creature was running on top of the water. Bill shone the light in the direction from which the sounds had come. A string of bubbles floated slowly downstream.

"Are there any alligators in here?" Bill asked, in a controlled voice.

"You know there aren't," I replied.

"Uh-huh."

We moved on in the silence. The only sounds were those of the water breaking around us.

Reaching the other side at last, we found our way blocked by impenetrable brush. Thorns tore at our clothes and scratched our bear arms and faces. We inched our way downstream to where the rocks meet the river. I tried to climb out but it was no use. The loose flakes of limestone crumbled in my hands, sending me crashing into the inky darkness.

Back into the river we went. The water was neck deep at this point. Something brushed against my leg. "Probably just a shad," I reassured myself. I paused for a moment, then moved on. My boot came up against something hard—a concrete step. We had found the trail which, at this point, was under five feet of muddy water.

We scrambled up the bank and sat down to catch our breath. Our camera cases, like ourselves, were covered with mud. At that moment we could have been the only two people on earth. The silence was absolute. Unseen canyon walls towered above us in the night.

We began working our way along the steep trail. The eerie darkness absorbed our light like a sponge. There was no wind, no cicadas...and no copperheads. Evidence of high water was everywhere. The loose sand, which before had covered everything, had all been washed away. The bank likewise had been torn by the floodwaters and piles of brush were strewn in its wake.

After more than an hour of fruitless searching, we turned back. Bill jarred the flashlight a couple of times, but it was no use. Realizing we had left our fresh batteries back at the car, we knew we were now without light. We groped our way back down the steep trail and out into the murky water.

It was well after midnight when we finally found our way back to where we had left the car. Having lost our way on the return crossing, we had become hopelessly mired in the muck. I had even lost the heel of my left boot trying to extricate it.

Once back on the road things started looking up. Unlike the earlier trip, there were plenty of snakes on the road this night. We had seen two large diamondbacks before reaching the turn-off to Castolon. A spotted night snake gave us a merry chase before we finally managed to catch, photograph and release it. We drove on two more miles. Bill hit the brakes suddenly, then spun the car around. A black-tail had just started to crawl up onto the roadway; if not for Bill's quick reflexes we would have missed it.

Two more diamondbacks, both juveniles. One of them had evidently been run over, although there were no external signs of injury. I entered in my field notes: No. 1576, D.O.R. We continued, the black highway blending into the darkness ahead of us. As if from nowhere, a snake appeared in the glow of our headlights. It was about four feet long. The tail, tapering to a point at the tip, told me that this was no rattlesnake. I had the door opened and one foot on the ground even before Bill could get the car stopped. The large eyes and bold H-shaped markings down the middle of its back left no doubt whatsoever in my mind. This could only be one thing: a trans-Pecos rat snake! A rare find even here where they are considered much more common than in other parts of their range. It goes without saying that this was a welcome addition to our ever-growing list of species. I examined the snake carefully, especially its tail. Specimens encountered here in the Big Bend are often infested with a highly specialized variety of tick (*Aponomma elaphensis*) which appears to be "host-specific" for this particular species of rat snake. Heavy infestations may result in the loss of the tail tip, a phenomenon reported by Bill and Paula Degenhardt (Southwestern Naturalist, 10:167-178, July 1965). Close examination, however, revealed that this particular snake was not parasitized. Like the previous snakes, it was photographed and released.

Still cruising, we turned west towards Study Butte. Two more diamondbacks and another black-tail; by now we were well out of the park. Although the hour was late, there was still plenty of activity on the roads. From Lajitas to Presidio, which means "penal colony," the road parallels the Rio Grande. This is a favorite stretch for commercial collectors—delightful individuals who, in my estimation, have all the moral scruples of a bounty hunter.

We stopped for a small snake in the road that turned out to be a glossy snake. Releasing it a safe distance from the roadway, we drove on. Another small snake: a rat snake, again! I could hardly believe my eyes. I picked the little snake up and held it in my hands, then turned it over to reveal the mother-of-pearl opalescence of its belly. This was an exceptionally fine specimen. It is generally acknowledged that "subocs" from Texas tend to be drab, often lacking the sulfur yellow ground color seen in New Mexico specimens. Another diamondback, one more "glossy" and a "D.O.R." black-tail. I glanced at my watch; it was 2:30 a.m. By now Bill and I were both having trouble keeping our eyes open. Arriving in Presidio, we found our way to a dingy little white-stuccoed building with one dim bulb for a porch light and a pretentious sign proclaiming it as *the* "Hotel."

We entered the front door and rang the bell for service. The proprietor, a matronly Spanish lady who spoke no English—at least not in our presence—glared disapprovingly. Covered with mud from head to foot, our eyes bloodshot from endless hours of road cruising, bleeding and barefoot from our canyon adventure, we just stood there.

The woman spoke to Bill, who looked at me and shrugged his shoulders.

"I think she wants to know if we work around here," I explained.

"Oh, no ma'am," Bill said with a friendly grin. "We're just a couple of tourists."

On the way home, Bill and I stopped at one of those "tourist traps" along the highway, this one just outside White City. In addition to the usual assemblage of confections and memorabilia including rattlesnake ashtrays, cactus candy, print bandannas and feathered headdresses, they also had a collection of live reptiles which could be seen for a nominal fee. I was somewhat surprised to find that the collection included both a Gila monster and a trans-Pecos rat snake, both protected species in New Mexico.

Among the exhibits one normally expects to find in such a place was a "wishing well" with its usual complement of rattlesnakes, ranging in size from two to five feet and long since resigned to the hail of coins of various denominations (and weights) which was inevitably showered upon them by naive and thoughtless tourists. The idea is, of course, to throw money into the well and make a wish. Ostensibly, if the snake drinks, your wish will come true. Regardless of whether or not you are a believer, as often as not there is no water available for the snake to drink, rendering the entire question academic.

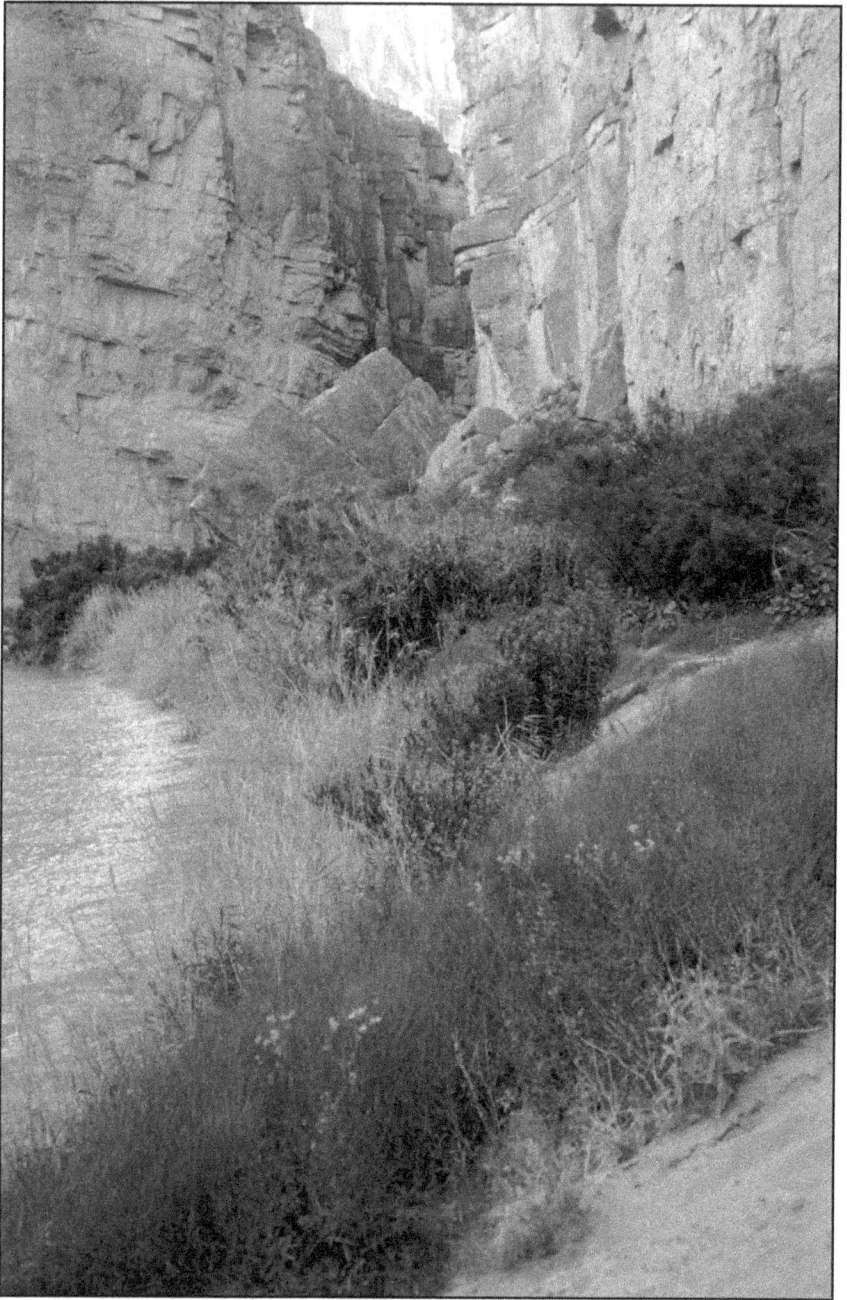

Santa Elena canyon, Big Bend Texas.

Trans-pecos rat snake

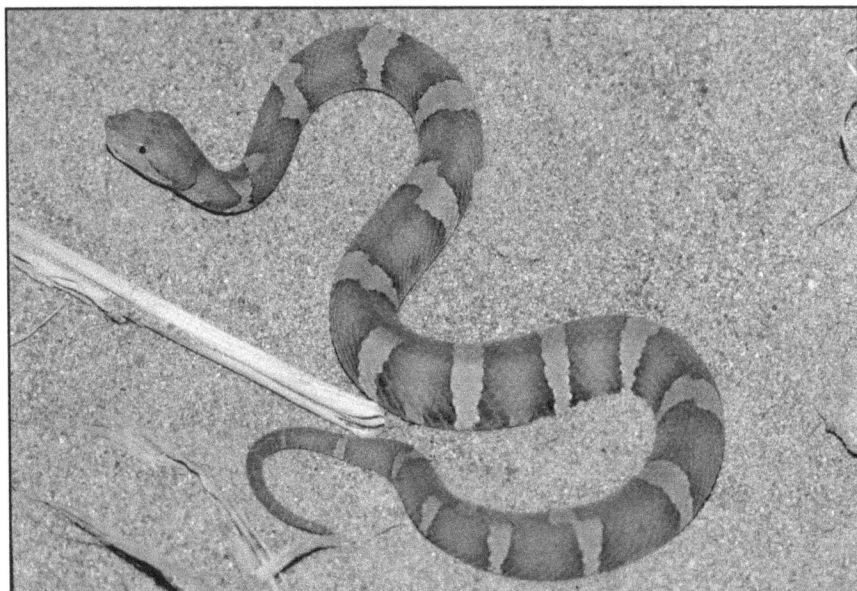

Big Bend copperhead

BAJA—LAND OF BOJUMS AND BEACHES

The Baja peninsula extends some seven hundred miles south from the California mainland separating the Sea of Cortez from the Pacific Ocean. Indigenous to the peninsula are many unique and interesting creatures, including the extremely rare Santa Rosalia rat snake, which, so far as I know, has never been exhibited in a live collection anywhere.

My mission was to find and photograph this elusive species. I had arranged to meet with a group of wildlife biologists from the United States National Fish and Wildlife Service who were generally familiar with the area in question and who had spent several years conducting faunal surveys in the region. The head of this task force was a friend of mine from my undergraduate days, Dr. Mike Bogan. The "resident" herpetologist was Bob Reynolds, with whom I was also acquainted, a congenial and capable field researcher. Accompanying me on the trip was my "comrade in arms," Doug Duerre.

Shortly after dawn on April 15, 1980, Doug and I piled our gear into his 4x4 pick-up and headed for the land of beaches and Bojums— Baja California, Mexico!

Our Baja sojourn was fraught with misfortune from the outset, even before we crossed over the international boundary at Nogales. Doug and I had taken a short side trip into Madiera Canyon in the Santa Rita Mountains located halfway between Tucson and the Mexican border. So intent were we upon photographing the local flora and fauna that we had become separated somewhere along the trail.

I was trying to photograph an unusually handsome male Yarrow's spiny lizard. The lizard, shy about having its picture taken, retreated under a rock. I reached down, thinking that I might flip over the rock and snap a picture before the lizard darted away. No sooner had I touched the rock than I felt a burning pain in the middle finger of my right hand.

The pain was immediate and intense. I was totally dumbfounded. As I returned the mile and a quarter back down to the parking lot, the pain began to spread up my arm. I was also aware of a tingling sensation in my hands and feet. Two tiny white doughnut-shaped markings now appeared on the inside proximal aspect of my finger.

I described my experience to Doug over a can of pears, having managed the can opener with great difficulty. He was very curious and suggested that we hike back up the trail to where I had last seen the lizard.

Once there, Doug, using a stick and a certain amount of discretion, flipped over the rock. There we saw not one but two scorpions—Centuroides! We did not know whether one had stung me twice or, less likely, they had each stung me once. At the time it really didn't matter one way or the other. I had never dreamed a scorpion sting would be so painful.

I began to have stomach cramps and trouble with my vision. My eyes twitched uncontrollably. The thumb and index finger of my right hand likewise twitched. The sting had occurred at approximately 4:30 p.m., and by 7:30 the pain in my arm had started to spread to my shoulder. I developed a sore throat and was having a great deal of trouble swallowing.

By 8:00 p.m. I began to have chills and, at Doug's insistence, agreed to call the hospital in Nogales. In fact, Doug refused to cross the border unless I agreed to see a doctor first. By now I was experiencing pain in all my joints and was becoming somewhat disoriented. I tried drinking some milk, but it felt like gravel in my throat.

I called the hospital. The nurse was reassuring. She told me I was having an unusually severe "allergic" reaction and could die! She then added thoughtfully that they could give me an antidote, and I should be all right within a few hours. It sounded like the only sensible thing to do. However, upon arrival at the hospital I was told they were all out of the required medication; all they had left was some "snake bite medicine" (antivenin? for a scorpion sting?). No thanks.

They kept me under observation for several hours, said there was nothing else they could do for me, suggested that I stay in town for the night in case I stopped breathing, presented me with a bill for sixty dollars, and said good-bye; with a smile!

I shuffled back to the car. We were supposed to rendezvous with our wildlife biologist friends from the Washington office three days hence in La Paz. I was beginning to have my doubts. We got a motel room for the night. I dozed off a couple of times, but was soon awakened from the pain in my now swollen but otherwise unremarkable hand.

The following morning was a repeat of the night before. I had no sense of touch in my hands or feet, making it impossible to manipulate objects and allowing me to walk only with great difficulty. The tingling sensation had spread to my legs, face, scalp and ears. I had to force myself to swallow and could not see well enough to distinguish between a carton of milk and a container of orange juice. My chest and shoulders ached, and I was short of breath.

We left Nogales at 9:00 a.m., stopping only long enough to have our entry permits validated and to fill our gas tanks. The filling station attendant handed Doug a stack of coins in change. "Para su cajita," he said with a grin. Doug nodded obligingly and we were off.

Aside from a few detours due to road repair we made good time, arriving in Guaymas before sundown. I spent another restless night in a beach front hotel. The following morning we took the ferry across to Santa Rosalia, a seven-hour trip. Vendors aboard the craft displayed hand-woven hammocks and ironwood statues carved by local Indians. I lay back on my bunk watching the reflection of the waves playing across the ceiling of my cabin.

As we approached Tortuga Island we were entertained by a

pod of porpoises playing tag in the wake, while pelicans dove into the water after fish—following one another like so many fighter planes in formation. Then began our long drive to the tip of the peninsula. I couldn't see well enough, so Doug did all of the driving.

Darkness closed in. Somehow, we inadvertently managed to get off the main highway and onto a narrow dirt road. We had no idea where it was taking us. It wound along between seemingly endless rows of palm trees and ocotillo fences. We were clearly lost. Then suddenly, in the middle of nowhere, we found ourselves in the garden of a grand hotel. A group of troubadours sang ballads on the lawn next to a pool. A waiter with a towel over his arm approached us and inquired if we would be "staying for dinner." I just wanted to take a hot shower and go to bed. This was the thriving metropolis of Mulege' (pronounced "Mule-a-hay"), population 4,000. Where they all lived, I don't know. All I had seen was a few scattered huts.

We were up early the following morning. We still had a long drive ahead of us. As we prepared to leave I noticed that the hotel even had its own private landing strip!

We drove south along the coast, stopping in Loreto to talk with a Senior Rodriguez about the possibility of chartering a boat to take us to "la Isla Carmen." We had considered stopping here on our return trip, in the hopes of finding the indigenous little rattlesnake, *Crotalus enyo*. We were told that the charge for two persons for two nights would be $80.00 U.S.—not unreasonable.

Ten miles south of Loreto we picked up a beautiful gopher snake, with the reddish color characteristic of this particular subspecies. We crossed over the Sierra de la Giganta, arriving in Insurgentes by late afternoon.

Turning south we encountered two hitchhikers—father and son—going in our direction. They seemed happy to accept a ride in the back of our pick-up. But to the great surprise of our passengers, we had gone only a little distance when I suddenly spun the truck around and headed back in the direction from which we had come. To their relief, I stopped the truck along side the road, got out and rescued a young horned lizard which, confused by the traffic, seemed to be having difficulty finding its way off the highway. Our new friends laughed with relief and pointing to our catch they said, "Camaleon. . . camaleon. . .," repeated several times for our benefit. It was sunset when we dropped them off in Constitution.

A snake was stretched out in the middle of the highway. I swung the truck around and opened the door to get a better look. I couldn't believe my eyes. The head was definitely that of a Mitchell's rattlesnake (or speckled rattlesnake). The body had a beautiful speckled and unmistakably Mitchell's appearance. The tail, however, exhibited the typical black and white banded pattern which I had come to associate with the western diamondback. I reached down carefully and placed it in one of the muslin sacks. Too much traffic to photograph it here; we would have to wait until we could find a safer place to pull off the highway. I recalled that the Mitchell's, like the sidewinders, derive most—if not all—of their moisture from the food they eat.

A tiny snake darted across the road ahead of us. It was distinctly banded with a cylindrical body—a banded sand snake. Taxonomically, this snake was of some interest because it was from a gap in the known range and sheds light on the nature of geographic variation in this species. Two more miles; another small snake, this one with a black head, darted out onto the road. Naturally, a black headed snake. We were in very high spirits by now. Our first day on the peninsula and we already had five different species.

We came to a spot where an arroyo crossed the highway. This would be a good place to take some pictures. We photographed the two small snakes first. Then came the big disappointment. As I opened the bag containing the Mitchell's, I saw that its mouth was open and the snake was in a contorted position. Close inspection revealed that it had been run over, a casualty of the automobile wars. Aside from an apparent lethargy, I had been unaware of any irregularity of its condition at the time of collection. The only visible external evidence of injury was a scrape along the side, displacing three or four scales. The Fish and Wildlife people would be glad to get it anyway.

By now it was 8:55 p.m. and the temperature was beginning to drop. I glanced at the thermometer; seventy-five degrees. The only other snake we saw on the road that night was a "D.O.R." patchnose.

We arrived in La Paz at ten o'clock that night. Accommodations were minimal. We got a motel room with no lock on the door but we were too tired to care. A quick meal out of a can and we turned in for the night.

We arrived at the airport at 9:30 the next morning, half an hour ahead of schedule. No Fish and Wildlife people in sight. At the desk we were told that the flight we were to meet had been canceled. There would be another at 11:00. We decided to wait, since there didn't really seem to be much choice. Eleven o'clock came and went, but still no sign of Fish and Wildlife. We lingered for a while about the airport parking lot and just as we were about to give up hope, I spotted a Department of Interior "carry-all." With a sigh of relief we were soon on our way to the Fauna Silvestre research station at Todos Santos.

About three miles south of Todos Santos we left the highway and took an "improved" dirt road. The dust was so thick I could hardly see to drive—and when I could see, it didn't help much. We were now driving precariously close to the rim of a huge "barranca." At one point, visibility was so bad I nearly went over the edge before I realized I was no longer on the road.

At La Burrera Canyon we found the Camp Chief ("C.C."), Mike Bogan, and the "A.P.H." (All-Purpose Herpetologist), Bob Reynolds, tagging and preserving specimens while other members of the crew were transcribing "meaningful and copious notes" into their logs. Bob reached into a jar and withdrew his hand. A young rat snake!

Bob explained that he had picked the snake up in the Sierra de la Giganta, on the outskirts of "Comondu Viejo." The ring of scales extending beneath the eye showed its close affinity to our own trans-Pecos rat snake, apparently its only close relative. My only regret was that I didn't have the opportunity to see and photograph it in its own natural setting.

I asked Mike what they hoped to accomplish here. "Quite simply," Mike explained, "we are trying to gain a better understanding of the systematics and distribution of small mammals and reptiles of the area." He went on to explain that they worked closely with the Fauna

Silvestre, but that the Mexican government had only one full-time wildlife biologist on the entire peninsula. It may have been that their presence here was also in keeping with a policy of improved relations between governments.

After lunch Doug and I decided to have a look around the area near camp. The sky was overcast—hazy but not cloudy. We crossed a dry arroyo which Bob assured me was a full-fledged river during the rainy season (recalling that we were now south of the Tropic of Cancer), and began to scale the bank on the far side. We progressed cautiously, as even the larger rocks were easily dislodged. This is the habitat of the rock lizard; one of the largest, by far the prettiest, (with its contrasting pattern of black, turquoise and yellow) and certainly the most evasive lizard on the entire peninsula. However, seeing the lizards from a distance is one thing; getting close enough to capture one is another. While I could excuse my lack of rubber-band skill on the numbness of my hands and blurring of vision, from which I still had not fully recovered, Doug had no such affliction to fall back on; for him this was a humiliating experience.

Time after time we would approach an outcrop of rock, one of us from each side. Time after time we would make our ascent, reaching the top of the rock only to see the lizard we were pursuing disappear into a crack. Once or twice I managed to knock one off the rock with my No. 105 rubber band, only to have it hit the ground running! Their endurance is amazing.

That night Bob joined us for some road cruising but several miles turned up nothing. A cold front was moving in and a dry, cool breeze was blowing through the canyon. Two hours later we returned to camp. We had seen only three jackrabbits and one scorpion. Just five months earlier, Bob assured us, this canyon had been teeming with "red diamonds, lyre snakes and rosy boas."

The following morning the sky was heavily overcast. A trail of smoke drifted up from the dying campfire. In the gray light of dawn I could see the silhouette of a cardon cactus towering above me. The distant sound of a bell drifted in on the still morning air and an occasional dove could be heard somewhere off in the distance. As I started to roll over I felt a sharp pain in my heel. The fine needles of the cardon littered the ground—literally by the millions. They could only be seen by deliberate inspection. My bedroll contained thousands of the hairlike spines!

After breakfast Doug and I resumed our efforts to capture the wily *Petrosaurus*. By noon we had managed to secure two—one adult and one juvenile.

In the process we made a curious observation. All of the smaller lizards and some of the larger ones had yellow eyes, while a few of the larger individuals had red eyes. We mentioned this to Bob, who said he had also observed this phenomenon but was so far unable to give a satisfactory explanation for it. Red eyes did not appear to be an example of sexual dimorphism, as it occurred in individuals of both sexes.

We left shortly after dark that night on the long drive back to La Paz. It was too cold for road cruising. But as far as Doug was concerned, the trip was already a success: he'd managed to capture and photograph the elusive *Petrosaurus*...alive!

The following day, at Doug's suggestion, we stopped at a culvert about fifteen miles northwest of La Paz—a worthwhile stop, as it turned out. Within twenty minutes Doug had produced four genera, representing four different species, two of which occurred only in southern California. These included the orange-throated whiptail, side-blotched lizard, leopard lizard and leaf-toed gecko. The latter is a remarkable species with highly specialized feet. The toe pads, like those of many geckos, are adapted for clinging to seemingly smooth surfaces—even glass. The ease with which these remarkable creatures can walk upside down across a plaster ceiling, for example, had baffled the minds of scientists for decades.

It was not until the advent of the electron microscope that the secret of their acrobatic antics became fully understood. Transverse ridges on the bottom of each pad support tiny hair like filaments. Each "hair" is bifurcate at the tip, each branch terminating in a microscopic suction disc. Once again we find nature has preempted man's own ingenuity.

A second stop down the road netted a tree lizard of a variety not found in the United States, and a young spiny lizard. These last two species were both found on the fallen trunk of a cardon cactus—the tree lizard once again demonstrating the remarkable versatility of camouflage for which this species is noted.

The aforementioned lizards were all placed in zip-locked plastic bags in our ice chest to reduce the risk of their escape while being photographed and to render them more easily posed.

Several miles south of Constitucion we spotted a large, black snake stretched out motionless across the highway. As we slowed the truck to a stop, we saw that it, too, had been hit. It was a black coachwip—in excess of five feet, and stout. A closer inspection revealed a recently ingested rattlesnake—a red diamond and in perfect condition. We photographed both.

It was dark when we reached the Sierra de la Giganta. Cool air flowed from the canyons out across the beach. I checked the thermometer: sixty-six degrees and still falling. "A little chilly for snakes," I thought. Just then I saw the fluorescent shine of a partially-coiled snake on the left-hand side of the roadway. A second Mitchell's rattlesnake, identical in all respects to the first—and also a road-kill.

The road turned north and we passed the spot where we had found the bullsnake. It was approaching midnight as we passed Bahia Concepcion. We passed a sign which, loosely translated, explained that this highway was built for the purpose of economic development, not for high speed transit. Obviously the bus drivers don't bother to read. The Kamikaze truckers likewise paid little attention to incidental highway signs; a fact on which we were inclined to blame many of our disappointments on this and other nights of road cruising.

We arrived in Mulege shortly before 2:00 a.m. and bedded down for the night. The next morning we drove leisurely north towards Santa Rosalia, stopping along the way to photograph the scenery which, everywhere in Baja, is outstanding—emerald waters, white sandy beaches, palm trees; cardon cactus!

In Santa Rosalia our first stop was to verify our reservations at the ferry dock. Here we were told we should have been there the night before. We explained that we had made reservations upon arrival, but our arguments were to no avail. We would just have to wait. The next ferry was not scheduled to leave until 11:00 p.m. on the 24th.

The next morning we continued driving south along the beach. At Bahia Concepcion we hunted lizards in the rocks high above a blue lagoon. The cool wind and overcast skies discouraged much in the way of activity. Even the side-blotched lizards, noted for their indifference towards the seasons, were absent.

Our last day on the peninsula we tried our luck in the other direction. Following a delay of over an hour due to a funeral procession, which wound its way in and out among the dusty streets of Mulege, we were finally able to drive north along highway 1, stopping in the vicinity of Tres Virgenes. Here we split up. I had been walking for about forty-five minutes without seeing anything other than a couple of young whiptail lizards, when a white object attracted my attention. I knelt down and picked it up. It was a piece of bone, but very curious. It looked like the flat rib of a large turtle. But what would a turtle be doing here? Looking around me, I now saw what must have been the remains of dozens of turtles—sea turtles! Hawksbills, to be precise. I had stumbled onto a poacher's camp. "Tortoise shell" still brings high prices on the international market. I took a picture and left.

When I finally caught up with Doug, he displayed a beautiful banded rock lizard—about seven inches long, with a banded tail and single black collar. We both took numerous photographs before releasing it, without realizing that it was a range extention.

We spent the rest of the afternoon making sure that our reservations were in order and that we wouldn't get left behind again. Once on board the ferry, we relaxed.

From the time we landed in Guaymas until we arrived in Albuquerque we made only one stop. I couldn't go through Sierra Vista without seeing Nell. As we crossed over into New Mexico, a strange green glow appeared in the sky over the Chiricahuas. A ball of fire seemed to hover for a moment and then disappeared behind Barfoot Peak. The unusual was commonplace here: ball lightening, meteorites—even ghosts—are all taken in stride among the rugged peaks and deep canyons of the Sierra Madre.

Mike Bogan, Todos Santos camp, Baja California del Sur, Mexico.

Wood gatherer, Baja California, Mexico

Rock lizard. These Gold, black and turquoise lizards are as beautiful as they are difficult to photograph.

Doug Duerre examines a D.O.R. Mitchel's rattlesnake, Baja California Del Sur, Mexico.

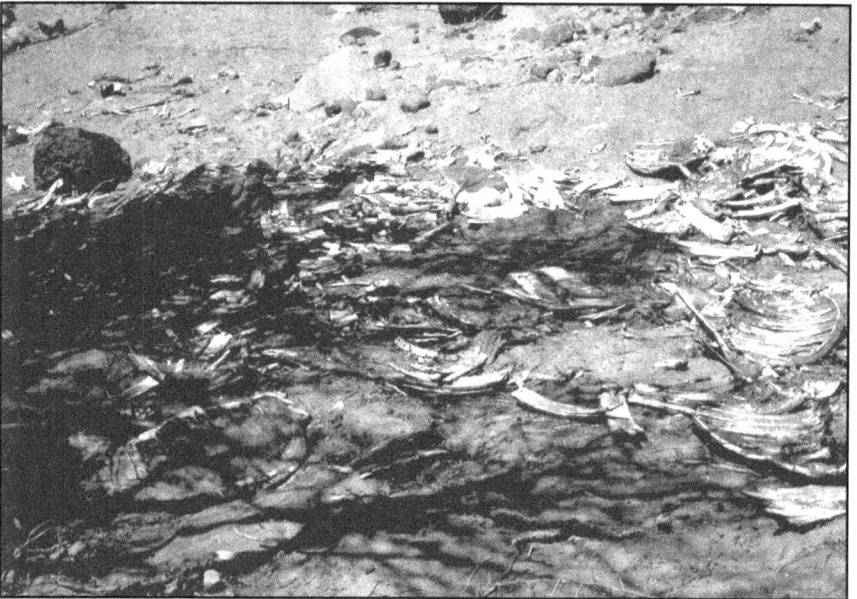

Poachers camp. Bones of hawksbill turtles cover the ground. Baja California del Sur, Mexico.

ANIMAS—MOUNTAIN OF SPIRITS

Far to the south, along the Continental Divide, the high peaks and canyons of Hidalgo County, New Mexico, contrast sharply with the surrounding desert. Just seventeen miles north of the international boundary stands Animas Peak, its precipitous rock face rising nearly eighty-six hundred feet above sea level. The unique physiography of the area and its geographic proximity to Mexico have combined to produce an ecosystem which rivals that of the Florida Everglades in the variety of plants and animals found there. This extraordinary array of wildlife is largely due to the influence of the Sierra Madre Occidental, a rugged mountain chain which forms an unbroken link with the cloud forests of southern Mexico.

Walnuts, sycamores and deciduous oaks thrive in the cool shade of the canyon bottom, characterizing the "lower encinal," while mountain mahogany, chihuahua pine and evergreen oaks, characteristic of the "upper encinal," seem to prefer the exposed slopes. This combination of floral elements includes remnants of the once-great Madro-tertiary forests which reached their maximum distribution during the Miocene epoch. The subsequent formation of North American deserts forced the retreat of these elements to higher elevations, where they remain to this day.

Like the plants with which they are associated, relict populations of animals also retreated to the safety and isolation of the mountains, each pursuing its own independent evolutionary path irrespective of the others, in response to subtle variations of climate and habitat, and each isolated by the surrounding desert just as surely as are the finches of "Darwin's archipelago" distinct and isolated, one from another.

The unique fauna of the area includes—in addition to an occasional jaguar—coatimundi, javelina, and the distinctive spotted bat. Unusual bird life includes the coppery-tailed trogon, groove-billed ani, Ridgeway's whippoorwill, whiskered owl, thick-billed kingbird and acorn woodpecker. Unusual amphibians are the sheep frog and green toad. Among indigenous reptiles we find the poisonous gila monster; the beautifully colored Sonoran coral snake, boldly marked with alternating bands of white, black and scarlet; and rarest of them all, the ridge-nosed rattlesnake.

The Animas Mountains (the old Spanish name, meaning "mountain of spirits") were at one time included in the Coronado National Forest. They are now privately owned and are off limits to trespassers, affording some measure of protection from obstreperous intruders and careless campers.

It was not until 1953, when a rider in the area reported finding a small, gray rattlesnake near the top of Animas Peak, that this obscure and secretive crotalid first came to the attention of the scientific community. At first it was thought that the small snakes were probably twin-spotted rattlesnakes, a species which we have noted is not uncommon in the Chiricahua Mountains, some fifteen air miles to the northwest.

In 1957 Robert Zeller, then a geologist with the U.S. Geological Survey, who was working along the international boundary, sent two examples of the small rattlers to the American Museum of Natural History; there they were immediately recognized by Dr. Charles M. Bogert to be members of the ridge-nosed group, a polytypic, predominantly Mexican species, so named because of the unique configuration of scales around the snout.

The Animas population was at first thought to be a northern

population of the Chihuahuan ridge-nosed rattlesnake by its comparatively drab appearance and lack of facial embellishments which are distinctive trademarks of the Arizona form.

There was little disagreement among members of the scientific community that, in the U.S., the Chihuahuan ridge-nosed rattlesnake is rare and probably always has been so, at least in "recent" times. Increased demand by commercial collectors, however, who had long since recognized the distinctiveness of the Animas population, had become cause for increasing concern among the more serious herpetologists.

Their reckless and overzealous collecting not only decimated the already restricted population, but their total disregard for the environment was also becoming a major factor in the loss of available habitat. Something would have to be done, and done quickly. Time was running out for the Animas Mountains ridge-nosed rattlesnake.

Among those first to become alarmed at the tenuous circumstances of the ridge-nosed rattlesnake in New Mexico was Dr. William G. Degenhardt, professor of herpetology at the University of New Mexico. In fact, that the Animas form was not officially recognized as a valid subspecies until as late as 1977 was largely due to apprehension on the part of Dr. Degenhardt and others, including myself, that formal recognition would further contribute to collecting pressure brought about by already inflated market prices. This problem was compounded by strenuous efforts on the part of far sighted persons responsible for legislation and law enforcement in the neighboring state of Arizona, efforts which had already brought about increased collecting pressure on certain reptile species, including this one, in New Mexico.

The effort to save the Animas ridge-nosed rattlesnake from extinction received an added boost in 1974 with the passage of the "Gross Bill," so named for its sponsor, New Mexico State Senator Fred Gross. This legislation directed the State Game Commission to "conduct studies to determine the status and requirements for the survival of endangered species" within New Mexico and to "establish programs... for the management of endangered species."

Also included was a clause providing monies from the state's general fund to support such programs. In preparing the list the Game

Department relied heavily on the proceedings of a regional symposium on rare and endangered non-game vertebrate wildlife, in which both Dr. Degenhardt and I participated. Although I had been invited specifically to present a paper on the Gila monster, I was keenly interested in the fate of our obscure little rattlesnake from the Animas Mountains.

Guidelines were established for the compilation of the New Mexico endangered species list, and a task force was assigned to prepare it. By January, 1975, the group had completed a preliminary list which, in March of that same year, was adopted by the Game Commission. Included on it was the "New Mexico ridge-nosed rattlesnake, *Crotalus willardi silus*" (later changed to *C. w. obscurus*).

Despite its recent protection and inaccessibility, federal officials anticipated an increase in collecting pressure. It was for this reason that the present study had been initiated. Funded through the U. S. Fish and Wildlife Service under the auspices of the Office of Endangered Species, and conducted under the direction of Dr. Degenhardt, the principal investigator for the study, a team of University of New Mexico scientists was assiduously collecting data on the ecological status of this unusual crotalid.

So it was, on a cloudy afternoon in May of 1975, I found myself in the office of my old friend and former professor, Bill Degenhardt. Bill spoke with dignified enthusiasm as he described the project to me. "Many theories have been proposed to explain the evolutionary and ecological implications of island populations," he explained. "These mountains provide an excellent model for testing those theories. If only for this reason, their indigenous populations should be considered a valuable resource. Regardless, the extinction of any species can have unforeseen and irreversible consequences, and should be avoided whenever possible."

Of course, the first step in such an ambitious program would be to determine something of the snake's distribution and population density, as well as to define its critical habitat in an effort to determine whether or not more stringent protective measures were indicated. Bill already had a team in the field working on this phase of the project. In fact, it was in the spirit of this endeavor that I soon found myself subjected to the indignities imposed upon unwary travelers in the New Mexico "outback."

Approaching from the north, I could not mistake the familiar outline of Animas peak. My companion and driver was Joe Shaw, a free-lance writer and journalist with the University of New Mexico Information Office. The "wagon" bucked and groaned as Joe maneuvered it over this misrepresentation of a road, terminating in Indian Creek Canyon, our destination. Attempting to navigate the numerous arroyos, Joe twisted and turned among tangles of mesquite, the thorns of which can easily puncture a tire.

The arroyos themselves constitute no particular problem during the dry season. In a matter of weeks, however, summer thunderstorms would invariably create flash floods, transforming these usually dry watercourses into raging torrents within minutes.

An added inconvenience, fist sized rocks constitute much of the road's surface and have the frustrating habit of knocking holes in gas tanks. For such emergencies I always carry an empty coffee can (the larger the better) and a tube of silicon aquarium sealant, which I have found affords a satisfactory seal.

Dust filtered through the open windows, settling on the seats and dashboard. As the car jolted along, Joe wheeled a hard left, guiding it up over a steep hump in the road. Besides an occasional windmill, the dominant features of the landscape here are yuccas and bear grass.

It was late afternoon when we arrived at "base camp." Roger Mongold and Steve Williams were attempting to tighten the guy ropes supporting one of the tents, while Bill Degenhardt and Warren L. Wagner, a graduate student at the University and botanist for the project, contemplated the damage done to a busted tail pipe on Bill's Land Rover. Steve, who had proved his field worth working with the endangered Jemez Mountains salamander, was teaching at the university at the time. Although not officially part of the project, he had managed to turn up an immature female ridge-nosed the previous season. Roger, likewise, had contributed a single female rattlesnake to the project after having spent several months in the field. Bill had collected an immature male that same day and, although this was my seventh trip to the

Animas, it was only the second "obscurus" I had seen in the wild.

It had been eleven years since Bill Brown, Mabel and I had first visited the Animas in the spring of 1964. It was on that memorable trip that I collected my first mountain kingsnake. Aside from the obvious signs of heavy use, the sights, sounds and smells of the canyon were still very much as I had remembered them.

That evening Roger and several other members of the crew made their usual supply run into Lordsburg, seventy miles away, for "provisions"...especially the "cerveza" which had become a camp staple during the long, hot days, weeks and months that Roger and his companions had spent in the canyon.

It was after dark before Roger and the others returned. Sitting around the campfire, those of us who had stayed behind listened to Bill as he discussed the events of the day and made plans for tomorrow. We spoke in low, hushed tones, as though we did not wish to disturb the sleeping spirits.

As I gazed into the glowing embers of the dying campfire, my thoughts returned to the snakes on the mountain. Here they had lived in harmony and seclusion for thousands of years. Looking up into the cloudless, star-studded sky, I wondered, "would they still be here ten years, fifty years, even one hundred years from now?"

In the morning, I was the first one about. Gathering some dry bark, I placed it over the still-smoldering campfire. There is something exhilarating about a pot of "sheep-herder" coffee brewing over an open campfire. As the smell of coffee wafted through camp, the others began to emerge. A cup of hot coffee and a cold boiled egg; we hurried through breakfast. The sun would be up soon, and we hoped to be well on our way by the time its life-warming rays penetrated to the canyon floor.

Gently I lifted the immature snake from its sack. As I did, I thought how easily this snake could have been mistaken for a dry oak twig. Almost reverently I held the delicate little snake between my fingers, then carefully marked him in the traditional fashion of scale clipping for later identification, and replaced him in my knapsack. With a motion from Dr. Degenhardt, we started up the trail. The robust form of a Clark's spiny lizard scampered up a nearby tree trunk as we passed.

We stopped to catch our breath at an outcrop of rocks where Bill had seen his very first "Willard's." Pressing on, we came to a place where the trail widens beneath a grove of long-needle pines. This was the "upper camp" which had been abandoned after Steve and Roger's encounter with a bear which had taken temporary possession of their sleeping tent—while they were in it!

Joe and I continued, pausing only long enough to take an occasional altimeter reading, passed "Turkey Spring" (also called "Aspen Spring") and finally came to our destination. Removing the young snake from its confinement, I released him in the exact location of his capture.

We then began retracing our steps to camp, giving in now and then to an irresistible urge to examine more carefully a likely looking clump of vegetation or inspect a fallen log that we might have overlooked during our ascent. At one point the trail narrows until it is necessary to force your way dense thickets of underbrush and an outcrop of rock extending from the canyon wall. A bush, just about head high, extended out into the trail. Joe brushed against it as he passed; I followed. I had just pushed my way through when I heard a short "bzzzzt." I turned to see Bill pointing to the center of the bush with his hook; there a large black-tail was coiled, waist high. Bill brought the snake out where it could be safely photographed, then continued on our way. Once again the black-tail had displayed its remarkably even temperament—for a rattlesnake.

As we were leaving, we turned to take one last look at Animas Peak, bathed in the golden glow of the late afternoon sun.

Several years later, John Applegarth and I collaborated on a survey of critical habitat of the ridge-nosed rattlesnake on public lands in southwestern New Mexico for the Bureau of Land Management. During the course of our field work I discussed the pros and cons of publicity as regards the species in question with Steve Dobrott, who was then the range management specialist and wildlife biologist for the Victorio Land and Cattle Company, an Arizona-based firm that owned and operates the Gray Ranch, headquarters of the company's operation in Hidalgo County. Actually the discussion was precipitated by Steve's reference to an article by Joe Shaw which he felt might encourage collecting activities on the mountain. I explained that collectors were already familiar with these mountains, and that commercial interests had long since recognized this race of rattlesnakes as distinctive, as evidenced in their price lists printed years before Joe's article had appeared. I felt it was our duty to inform the sympathetic public as to the uniqueness of this ecosystem through a concerted program of public education. Besides, regardless of our own philosophical biases, the public has a right to know.

It remained Steve's contention, however, that outside influences within so limited and fragile an ecosystem must be kept to a minimum. In all fairness I must say that he and his predecessors have done a good job managing the natural resources of the mountain and are to be congratulated on their spirit of cooperation and concern. My bottom line is that if we preclude all but a chosen few from experiencing the wilderness, we will have produced a generation unsympathetic to nature, unfeeling, indifferent—which will eventually destroy the very thing we sought to preserve.

Now John took a little getting used to. He'd come to UNM with a mission. His plan was simple, to set a record for taking longer than anyone else in the department to get a Ph.D. Towards this end he moved a cot into the museum and proceeded to fill one of the specimen cabinets with canned corn and Mazola; plenty of carb's for energy and most of the necessary amino acids? Under ordinary circumstances this might have just seemed peculiar, but John's dissertation involved digging up mummified bodies of animals and placing them in vats of Biz, which he stored in empty cabinets and closets throughout the museum. After several weeks a curious aroma began to flood the basement. People would come downstairs, turn and go quickly back up again; clutching their hand over their nose. "What's that smell?," they'd ask.

Months passed. More months passed. John informed his committee that he would require an "extension." The staff groaned. Needless to say, there was an aggregate sigh of relief from the basement when John finally did receive his degree. I guess my point is, when you worked with John, you just didn't get in a hurry. "No reason to rush."

Back at the ranch (literally), John and I, accompanied by Jim Bednarz, were about to witness a dramatic scenario of the never-ending struggle between predator and prey—this one made all the more dramatic in that *both* participants were predators.

It was early morning as we approached North Animas Peak in Jim's Land Rover. Crossing an arroyo, we had just begun climbing the steep bank on the far side. The spinning wheels churned up gravel and dust as the vehicle lurched forward. A sharp-shinned hawk, screaming as she came, swooped low over the hood of the Land Rover in a blur of motion and then began circling for another approach.

We were taken back by the suddenness and boldness of her attack. That is, until we realized that her aggression was directed not at us but at something unseen in a grove of trees just off to our left.

With a series of rapid wing beats the bird ascended and prepared for yet another dive. Searching the grove of oaks with our binoculars, we were able to make out what it was that had this bird in such a frustrated state of agitation. It was a young great-horned owl, no doubt intent on the three hawk chicks in the nest above our heads. The chicks, less than two weeks old, would be a delicacy for this young owl.

The mother hawk was safe for now, but come nightfall she would be helpless to defend her brood against the larger owl; of this we were well aware. This life and death struggle between a predator and its prey was somehow philosophically distasteful, and yet logic dictated that we should not intervene in the normal course of events. By now our very presence was compounding the problem. We had momentarily distracted the mother hawk's attention. It was possible that just by being there we might force her to abandon the nest.

The decision was made. We had to move on. It was shortly after 8:00 a.m. when we began our assault. We moved steadily upward, taking plant samples and photographs as we went. By ten o'clock we had reached the summit. Completing our task, we began our descent, again collecting vegetation samples along the way.

It was exactly twelve noon when we again approached the nest tree. The shrill screams of the mother bird told us the battle was on.

The blur of feathers again flashed past our windshield. We saw that the owl had left its cover and was again approaching the nest tree.

The mother bird was determined. She zeroed in, heading straight for the owl with deadly intent. Contact! Owl feathers flew in every direction. The owl himself was spun around by the force of the blow. The owl ducked his head, which swiveled like a turret of a tank, following the path of the hawk.

The next dive rolled the owl almost off its feet. We could see it was injured. It could neither escape nor attack. The inexperienced owl had proven no match for the provoked mother hawk. The hawk had won. The owl would die, but the hawk chicks would survive—at least for now.

We never did see a ridge-nosed rattlesnake, nor had we expected that we would.

Dr. William G. Degenhardt stands in the spot where he collected his first Animas Mtn. Ridge-nosed rattlesnake.

Animas peak, Hidalgo Co., New Mexico.

Michael Williamson displays a New Mexico ridge-nosed rattlesnake, Hidalgo Co, New Mexico. Photo by Paul Hyder

Joe Shaw, Indian Creek canyon, Hidalgo Co., New Mexico.

KOFA QUEEN

By the summer of 1981 there remained only one major group of native snakes not yet represented in the pages of my field notes. The "haenophidia" includes the world's largest snakes—the giant constrictors of Africa, Asia and South America. In the United States the group is represented by two somewhat less spectacular, seldom seen and little known forms: the rubber boa, an habitué of temperate rain forests of the northwest coast, and the rosy boa, an inhabitant of some of the remotest, barrenest, most desolate desert country imaginable.

Over the years my quest for this latter snake had taken me from the depths of Death Valley to the tip of Baja California. But this time I resolved that nothing would deter me from achieving my goal—to find and photograph this desert recluse.

So it was that in the spring of that year my companions and I hatched our boldest and most ambitious scheme. The plan called for us to make a journey that was to take us over two thousand miles in six days. The idea was to spend approximately two days in each of three locations we thought most likely to produce results: Death Valley, the Kofa Mountains, and Organ Pipe Cactus National Monument. We never made it.

On the second morning following our arrival in Death Valley we were to hunt the lower part of Hanapauh Canyon, one of several known rosy boa locations within the Monument. Leaving Furnace Creak early, we drove south across a harsh and forbidding landscape, which afforded a sharp contrast to the snow-capped Panamint Range that loomed in the distance, and crossed over the "Devil's Golf Course" about midmorning.

There was no hint of trouble until just after we passed Shorty's Well. More than two hundred feet below sea level, against the glare of the desert sun reflected off an endless ocean of salt crystals that stretches for miles across the desert floor, disaster struck! It began with a blowout of the left rear tire. Then, even before I could bring the car to a halt, steam spewed out from under the hood. We had not only broken a fan belt, but the flywheel damper had cut through the timing chain cover. We weren't going anywhere. To make matters worse, the nearest place where I could get the needed spare parts to make repairs was Phoenix, Arizona!

As the wrecker towed us past "Bad Water," we were reminded that the temperatures here are said to exceed one hundred thirty in the shade—"and there ain't no shade."

But six weeks later, Paul Hyder and I were once again headed towards the Kofas. The name "Kofa" is a contraction for the 1896 mining claim, "King of Arizona Mine," adopted by mapmakers for want of anything better to call this over-sized chunk of rock jutting out of the lower Colorado desert.

Arriving from the south, we saw the rugged crags of this desert range towering ahead of us. We paused briefly to fill our gas tank and refresh ourselves at "Stone Cabin," the only permanent habitation on highway 95 along the nearly one hundred mile stretch from Yuma to Quartzite.

Nine miles north of Stone Cabin we left the blacktop highway and began to navigate a passable dirt road leading up into the mountains. At the end of the road is a scraped out turnaround. From here a hiking trail leads up a gradual incline to a cleft in the precipice harboring a relict stand of isolated palm trees. From 1910, when the prospector-explorer John Ramsey first discovered the palms, until 1930, when the population was verified by botanists, such reports of oases in the desert were generally attributed to the hallucinations of prospectors that had been out in the sun too long.

Somewhere between the highway turnoff and the entrance to Palm Canyon is an almost indiscernible scratch in the dirt indicating the turnoff to Kofa Queen Canyon, our destination. Little more than a jeep trail, the road hooks sharply to the north and then veers east into the canyon—a truly spectacular display of geologic forces in interaction with the elements. Precipitous cliffs rise on each side as the canyon walls seem to close in. The infrequent visitor is likely to be treated to a rare performance of cliff-hanging dexterity, courtesy of the majestic desert bighorn sheep which frequent this range (estimated to number between two and three hundred individuals).

Arriving at "skull rock," a natural feature which, depending upon the angle of the sun and the extent of the observer's imagination, looks more or less like its name implies, we stopped to stretch our legs and have a look around. We were immediately greeted by a swarm of bloodthirsty gnats whose relatives I was sure I had met on an earlier trip to Tucson, and whose admirable persistence threatened to be our undoing. There was no escape. They buzzed about our ears and nostrils, crawled through our hair and beards, and even lodged themselves under our eyelids. To retreat to our vehicle was unthinkable; we would be done like a baked potato within minutes. There was nothing we could do but endure. Even our sticky insect repellant only deterred them briefly.

By 6:00 p.m. the temperature "in the shade" was still well into the nineties. The heat seemed to drive the gnats into a feeding frenzy. "Should be a great night for collecting," I interjected between slaps. We hiked up the canyon for about two miles—maybe less—and sat down to wait for dark. A bug crawled up a rock next to my leg. As Paul reached down to examine our somehow less than appealing visitor he informed me that this was a cone-nose bug, a rather common house pest in parts of the southeastern United States and added that they can give a rather nasty bite. I took his word for it.

Almost without noticing it, darkness was upon us. We began walking slowly down the canyon. Paul, to my right, was sticking close to the vegetation while I worked the open gravel of the main wash.

We'd been walking for perhaps twenty minutes when I heard Paul's voice. "I've got a `Trimorphodon'"; his voice was low and unemotional.

He had just seen the last three inches of its tail as it attempted to escape into a bush. It was a large adult male, with the boldest markings I had ever seen in this particular subspecies of lyre snake. The chocolate brown crossbars were split by light centers to form the unmistakable "triads" definitive of the species. The prominent lyre-shaped marking on the head and the large eyes with their elliptical pupils could leave no doubt as to identity of this snake. I noted that the crossbars were more closely spaced than those of the subspecies which I had infrequently encountered in the lower Rio Grande Valley of Texas and New Mexico. Although "rear-fanged" and armed with venom which will quickly paralyze a lizard, they are apparently innocuous to humans.

A red-spotted toad—a xeric-adapted species not uncharacteristic of habitats such as this—put in his appearance and was granted accommodation in my collecting bag; there would be plenty of time later for photographs.

Another twenty minutes or so, I almost stepped on a second lyre snake, this one a juvenile female trying to escape in the clumsy fashion characteristic of its kind when surprised on open ground. The contour of the snake was effectively disrupted against the rocky substrate; its sudden motion, however, had betrayed its presence.

It was approaching 1:00 a.m. Just a few hundred yards to go and we'd be in camp. Still no sign of a rosy boa. The unexpected bonus, however, of finding a pair of lyre snakes almost compensated for our lack of success with the rosys. *Another* lyre snake! This was becoming almost routine.

Early the following morning I caught a striped whipsnake in the brush along the edge of the arroyo, about two hundred yards above camp, and broke my finger in the process. It was worth it, though, as it turned out to be a substantial range extension for the species; extending the range some seventy miles to the southwest of the previously published known distribution.

So encouraged were we by our limited success, and so impressed with the uniqueness of this isolated environment, that I immediately began making plans for our second trip to the Kofas, one that I felt confident would only end in success! This time Paul and I were accompanied by Doug Duerre. It would be the first time that the three of us had been in the field together.

We chose our route carefully. Weather patterns dictated that we drive as far west towards Kingman as possible, then due south to our destination. There was a chill in the September night air as we as we drove south from Quartzite on highway 95 towards Stone Cabin and turned off onto the now familiar dirt road leading up into the mountains. The moon, which was approaching the quarter on the decline side of its cycle, had not yet risen.

The headlights swung back and forth over the rough terrain. Winding in and out among the saguaro and ocotillo, we bounced along. One ravine after another appeared suddenly before us. Without warning, Doug's heavily-laden pickup would drop from under us, only to come crashing up again on the far side. Finally we arrived at our campsite—a wide spot in the arroyo bottom, about a quarter of a mile above "skull rock," two and a half miles from the mouth of the canyon.

We established a comfortable camp with two sleeping tents and one large cooking tent, complete with mosquito-mesh sides and a tarpaulin roof for shade. As we finished setting up camp, the moon cast an eerie glow on the opposite canyon wall. We decided to get a good night's sleep and make an early start in the morning.

We were aroused by the sun which was already streaming down the canyon, making it uncomfortably warm in the sleeping tents. We hurried to dress. After a cold breakfast we decided to explore the lower part of the canyon.

Following a fifteen minute chase, Paul and I managed to photograph a young zebra-tailed lizard, which obligingly assumed its characteristic retreat posture, its body held high, tail curled to reveal the black and white bars on the under side which give the lizard its popular name.

We began drifting apart and I found myself a little ways behind the others. A large striped whipsnake made a sudden dash into the underbrush. I made no attempt to follow.

As I returned, Paul was absorbed in examining a fallen agave. So intent was he, poking and probing gingerly at the defunct plant with his hook, that at first I thought he might not have noticed me. *"Xantusia,"* he said without looking up.

He knelt down and began peeling off the leaves one by one, taking care not to stick himself on the sharp spines. I joined in and soon we had peeled the entire plant, much as one might peel a giant artichoke. Still no sign of the night lizard.

A side-blotched lizard dropped out of the remaining stalk and made a quick dash for cover. I reached out and snatched it before it could make good its escape. *"Trimorphodon food,"* I said jokingly as I popped the lizard into a bag. Paul continued raking through the remains of the agave in hopes that he might have missed something the first time. Sure enough!

"I got it," he said. I turned to see a tiny lizard, less than two inches long. The scales on the body were granular, while those on the head formed large protective plates. The body was beige with olive speckles. The head was a darker hue, with a light yellow stripe running through the eye.

A half-dozen agaves later and I, too, had one of these dwarflike saurians. This was an exciting find, as I had never before collected this particular family of lizard. Also, the xantusiids have always had a special appeal for me, being so small and yet so reminiscent of the giant varanids.

We continued searching the slope and soon had a total of four night lizards, one a juvenile no more than an inch long from the tip of its snout to the tip of its tail.

I thought I heard Doug's voice coming from a rock outcrop across the canyon. I strained to listen. I could faintly make out the word "chuckwalla." Minutes later I arrived at the spot, camera in hand. Doug's "chuck" was a large male. The head and shoulders were black, profusely speckled with red. The tail and hind quarters were sulfur yellow. The under surface was a bright red-orange, turning to brick red towards the rear; much more colorful than any that I had seen in California or Nevada. The lizard had so inflated its body that it could not be easily extracted from its hiding place. Seizing the tail firmly with one hand, Doug carefully removed the cap rock to reveal one very surprised, and bloated, lizard.

Mid afternoon temperatures were now in the upper eighties. It was getting too hot to hunt so we returned to camp. Besides, we wanted to be well rested before nightfall, as this was the time we would be most likely to encounter our *real* quarry; the rosy boa.

As jagged rocks cast long shadows up the canyon, my companions began to grow restless. Finally Paul announced that he thought he might just take a little stroll about the vicinity. Doug, too, thought that he might have a look around. Paul had seen an unusual cactus in fruit and wanted a photograph of it. The two of them sauntered off, leaving me to set up the camp stove. Suddenly I heard Doug come crashing through the brush. Rocks clattered at his feet as he charged into camp, shirtless. Actually, he had a shirt, he just wasn't wearing it. Instead he had it tied in a bundle attached to the end of an aluminum tent pole.

"Baby Mitchell's," he gasped without waiting to catch his breath.

He'd seen another, bigger rattlesnake up on the hill. I grabbed a couple of bags. Into one of them we dropped Doug's still buzzing shirt. The other I tucked securely under my belt. Doug led the way into a narrow side canyon where we were soon joined by Paul who had arrived to see what all the excitement was about.

We now found our way blocked by a dense tangle of vegetation. Time and again we drove onto the impenetrable tangles, only to be repelled by the flesh rending thorns. Too late we realized the nature of our impediment—an especially insidious variety of *Acacia* (a member of the mimosa family) known locally as "cat's claw mesquite" which, in this hot climate with its concomitant growing season, achieves the stature of a tree, very unlike the bushes I was used to seeing in New Mexico.

We inched our way forward, sometimes dropping to our hands and knees. At other times we hacked away at the stubborn vegetation with flailing snake hooks. Seconds ticked away that seemed like hours. After a few short minutes of searching we had found and bagged another Mitchell's, a good three-footer.

Back at camp, we gave our captives a thorough examination. These Mitchell's, with their faded pink bands against a mottled gray background, were vaguely reminiscent of ones I had encountered several years earlier in the rocky hills northeast of Kingman. We surmised that these two were a pair, and that the male (the smaller of the two) might have been actively pursuing the female. Female rattlesnakes—as well as other snake species—lay down a scent trail (technically referred to as pheromones) which the males can follow for great distances.

By now it was getting dark. After one more long look at our captives. We replaced them in one of our insulated holding boxes, checked our sacks for tears, tested our hand lights to be sure they were in proper working order, and spread out to our respective collecting areas.

I was optimistic. Perhaps it was due to the excitement of the day, or did I sense that this was going to be the night for which I had waited so long. It was pitch dark as I began walking slowly up the canyon, moving my light from side to side, keeping a careful watch for eye shines that might reveal the presence of a concealed snake.

I estimated that I had walked about a mile and a quarter. The canyon was widening and becoming more rocky. A maze of gullies crisscrossed the main course, making it more difficult to follow. I felt a draft of cool air moving down the canyon. Turning, I hesitated, then moved on, scouring the branches (I recalled reading somewhere that rosy boas are good climbers). Shadows danced back and forth to the movement of my light. I resumed working my light beneath the dense vegetation along both sides of the arroyo. I tossed my light over my right shoulder. Something shiny distracted me. About seven yards off, lying on a bare patch of ground halfway between two bushes...it didn't move. Could it have been just a stick? No, it was too shiny to be a stick.

There it was—a rosy boa! I reached down and gently lifted the timid little snake with my fingers. Only after I touched it did it turn to face me, exploring my hand with its restless tongue. It was a young female. At long last my search was at an end.

I examined my bag carefully, running my fingers along the entire length of the seam. I wanted to leave nothing to chance. The snake's tiny eyes stared up at the light. I tied the bag securely and dropped it inside my shirt for added safety, taking every conceivable precaution to ensure that no unfortunate circumstance befell my newfound friend. As I approached the darkened camp, the audible tones of my companions' voices told me I was the last to return. "Have any luck?" they inquired as I reached for the zipper on the tent flap.

"A little," I replied, trying to sound casual. I handed the bag to Paul and began fixing myself a cup of hot cocoa. The others shared my good fortune enthusiastically, with only a tinge of disappointment. As it turned out, mine had been the only snake collected during the evening.

The wind blew all night, but had subsided by morning. I was up early as usual. The others were still asleep, so I decided to take a hike up a small side canyon which cuts into the rim just a few hundred feet above camp. As I walked alone in the early morning shade, everything seemed quiet and peaceful. A junco landed on a mesquite only a few feet from my head. I paused to examine a cholla—easily recognized by its attenuated and cylindrical form, hence the popular epithet "cane cactus." In one species the branches are closely arranged with closely packed yellow spines giving it a fuzzy ("cuddly") appearance. It is often, therefore, referred to as the "teddy bear cholla," a name which, as many are unfortunate enough to discover, is not entirely revealing of its true nature. The particular variety in question is more often referred to, by those with some intimacy, as the "jumping cholla," owing to the multitude of testimonials attesting to its purported powers of dispersal on the human form. This belief, while admittedly much exaggerated, is not entirely devoid of the truth. The joints are loosely connected and may break off at the slightest provocation, leaving the unwary hiker with a rather unpleasant sensation—and the unenviable dilemma of how to remove the persistent barbed spines without being struck repeatedly by a seemingly endless supply in reserve.

I veered south across the main arroyo and eventually came to the mouth of Ten Ewe Canyon, a major tributary of Kofa Queen. I was hoping to surprise some tardy snake, which—caught away from its lair—had curled up under a rock or bush to avoid the early morning chill. I hiked along at a rapid pace, keeping a watchful eye for that telltale coil.

As the sun rose over my left shoulder I watched the shadow of the north rim move slowly down the rock face ahead of me. I walked on until I came to a fork, one branch continuing south, the other curving around to the west. I hiked for another hour or so and then began making my way back towards camp.

I eventually came to a place near the mouth of the canyon where it had cut through a dike, leaving two columns of rock rising like pillars, one on each side. As I walked along, absorbed in my own thoughts, I was startled by a pair of bighorn sheep clambering along the ridge formed by the dike.

I returned to camp just in time for breakfast. Doug, who was accustomed to taking a short walk before meals, returned—bag in hand. The bag writhed and twisted as though itself possessed of the life force. Whatever its occupant, it was obviously anxious to regain its freedom. Doug opened the bag to reveal a young striped whipsnake, indistinguishable, except for its size, from the one I had collected on the previous trip. The charcoal colored snake had a light stripe running the entire length of the body on each side, beginning just behind the eye. The chin and throat were white with black flecks, the underside of the tail a dull coral pink. The light stripe, bisected by a broken black line, was yellow anteriorly, fading to a buff white towards the tail. The nervous snake was alert to every movement, and not at all reticent about applying its needle-sharp but otherwise harmless teeth to a careless finger should the opportunity arise.

The gnats, scourge of our last trip, had (as we were soon to discover) been replaced by flies, which invaded our cooking tent in profuse numbers. Just how these happy creatures gained entrance and why, once inside, they seemed inexplicably unable to find their way out again remains a mystery to this day.

As the day dragged on, however, our curiosity soon turned to consternation. Early in the morning the torpid vermin gathered in great bundles at the corners of the tent so as to absorb heat from the sun. Thus warmed, the flies began to grow ever more restless. As the masses started to separate, we noticed that they seemed to come in two distinct varieties, distinguished at a glance by their size. The large, noisy ones that while away the hours buzzing about your face and ears—usually coming to rest on your upper lip—were one kind. Then there were the small ones which swarm by the thousands and practice their suicidal attacks, directed with uncanny accuracy, on your cup of hot chocolate. The more skillful among them can easily zip through the opening of a pull-top soda can without even brushing a wing.

Paul and I later hiked up "Mitchell Canyon," as we now called it, in the hope of improving our luck. On the way up we paused to examine a large barrel cactus. As we stood there, a large male rosy—which had evidently come from beneath a clump of scrub oak—appeared about six feet up the embankment in front of us. In broad daylight!

Paul dove on the snake, simultaneously smashing his knee into the cactus. He came up holding the snake high above his head in one hand, and holding his knee with the other. A smile was superimposed on the otherwise contorted features of his countenance.

It was a beauty. Dark metallic stripes on a cream ground color ran the entire length of the snake, the dorsal stripe extending to the tip of its snout. The tiny eyes with their elliptical pupils seemed absurdly small. The entire under surface was cream colored with flecks of the same metallic color that comprised the stripes. That this one was a male was attested to by the almost indiscernible spurs, one on each side of the vent, revealing the lizard ancestry of this ancient lineage. So many trips without success, and we now had a pair of rosy boas in less than twenty-four hours. It was hard to believe, but there they were. Back at camp we opened the bags; as if to reassure ourselves that we weren't going to wake up any moment and find it was all just a dream.

The only other remarkable find of the day was a black-tailed rattlesnake that Paul and I picked up later that evening in almost the exact same spot where Doug had found his first Mitchell's. This find was somewhat of a surprise, as it represented a range extension and the first record for the Kofas. In the dark, I had actually mistaken the banded snake for a lyre snake and might have picked it up had not Paul stopped me.

This snake, along with several collected earlier, would eventually find its way into the collection of the Smithsonian Institution in Washington D.C., via the Denver Wildlife Research Center's regional office at the University of New Mexico. Meanwhile it would be photographed and maintained for a period of observation.

The following morning we set out to photograph all of the "critters" that we had thus far not had an opportunity to photograph. Afterwards Paul and I made one more run up "Mitchell Canyon." A kit fox followed our movements from a small rise only a few yards to our left then trotted off at a casual pace. I was struck by the seeming lack of fear that characterized all animal life in the canyon.

The reptiles, if they were here, weren't moving. There seemed to be something—a change in the weather perhaps—but I'm sure that the animals sensed it too.

That night we tried to repeat our earlier successes but to no avail. Doug hiked for several miles above camp from late afternoon until well after dark, searching first one side of the canyon, then the other. He found the remains of a lyre snake which, judging from its parched condition, had been dead for a considerable period of time. Other than that and one chuckwalla extracted from beneath a cap rock, our search yielded nothing. Later we decided to break camp early the following morning. We had spent four nights and three days in the Kofas and those were memorable days.

On the way home we stopped at a series of isolated dunes a few miles northeast of Bouse, hoping to find a stray sidewinder or two. We arrived late in the afternoon and I almost immediately started tracking a young gopher tortoise. Its tracks in the sand showed distinctly the outline of each individual scale. The tracking was easy—that is, until the turtle decided to strike out across the "desert pavement," comprised of pebbles worn smooth and tightly packed to form a continuous surface.

I scanned the surrounding desert hoping to get a glimpse of the characteristic domed shell. I continued walking along the edge of the dunes in case the tortoise decided to wander back that way. The loosely packed sand was undermined by a maze of tunnels. Wherever a tunnel came too near the surface, the soft sand gave way, resulting in a moon shaped depression with a mound of sand at its center. These I began prodding gently with my stick. About the second or third one I heard a dull "thump" followed by a short hiss. I'd hit pay dirt! I plunged my hand into the soft sand and came out with a tortoise.

Its appearance was reminiscent of a small pineapple, the carapace being composed of dark hexagonal scutes, each with a yellow center. The cracked, dry skin gave it a much more ancient look than its estimated twelve-to-fourteen years indicated. It instantly drew into its shell, the head protected by two broad, flat forelimbs. These forelimbs are uniquely suited to another aspect of tortoise life. These dauntless diggers are known to construct long tunnels and to lay their eggs near the entrance where they are guarded against intruders, including marauding Gila monsters.

Although somewhat disheveled, this was a fine looking individual, truly prettier than any I had seen in captivity. Doug meanwhile had been chasing the local fringe-toed lizards, frequent inhabitants of the dunes, but with a notable lack of success in spite of his well earned reputation as a lizard hunter. The extent and complexity of the burrows made chasing these agile lizards almost an exercise in futility. Should Doug be so fortunate as to find one away from its tunnel entrance, it merely scampered over the crest of the nearest dune and disappeared beneath the sand without a trace.

Paul found a sidewinder track in the sand, but like the turtle tracks, it led out onto the desert only to vanish on the unforgiving surface of polished pebbles. It was, however, an enjoyable diversion and a pleasant ending to an otherwise spectacular trip.

Carmen Williamson makes a friend, a Nevada kingsnake

A hatchling desert tortoise takes his first glimpse of the outside world.

Mabel Williamson admires a desert tortoise.

Paul W. Hyder, Death Valley, California. Anyone familiar with Paul's work (Check out the picture of the green toad on page 157 of the field guide.) can agree that he sets the bar for field photography.

Sidewinder rattlesnake, Death Valley, California.

Death Valley, California.

Chuckwalla

Kofa Queen canyon, Yuma Co., Arizona.

Kofa Camp, Yuma Co., Arizona

Lyre snake, Kofa Mts., Arizona

Rosy Boa, Kofa Mts., Arizona

Skull Rock, Kofa Queen canyon, Yuma Co., Arizona

THE DUNES

Each of us has his own favorite collecting spot. For me it was the black-tail den; for Paul, the "dunes." The dunes are located about twenty-five miles south of Albuquerque, New Mexico, a pleasant half-hour's drive from town.

Lizards abound and snakes are plentiful enough. Nor are box turtles a rarity, and children as well as adults enjoy watching them pull into their shells, closing the "lid" securely. If one is patient, after a few minutes, after a few minute the hinged plastron (the lower shell) will open just a little and a wary eyeball can be seen peering out from within.

Only after ascertaining that all is well will the turtle suddenly extend its legs and make off in whatever direction the observer deems most unlikely. The turtles only occasionally bite, and children and pets soon learn to keep fingers—and noses—out of the danger zone. The ones with red eyes are the males; yellow eyes are females.

Paul will never forget the day he stopped to pick up a piece of "driftwood" which, to his great surprise, came suddenly to life and was about to escape into an indigo bush. It didn't take Paul any time at all to realize that this was a rare albino bullsnake—not just an ordinary albino either. The pattern was actually in relief! It is the only snake demonstrating this particular phenomenon that I have ever seen, before or since.

Besides box turtles and bullsnakes, other inhabitants of the dunes include the ever-present prairie rattlesnake and the feisty but harmless hognose—so called in reference to the upturned rostral scale which, although functional for burrowing in loose sand, gives the snake a quizzical appearance.

I recall one morning when I chanced upon one such individual while hiking along the margin near the south end of the dunes. So well did it blend in with the sand that I might easily have missed seeing the snake were it not for the sudden movement. Faded beige blotches ran the entire length of its stubby foot-long body. The snake lay motionless as I approached to make a closer inspection.

Suddenly it threw itself into a tight coil. Spreading its jaws and inflating its neck, the snake emitted a sharp "warning" hiss—a brave act for so small and defenseless a creature. It continued to thrash about, curling its tail first one way and then the other, exposing the bright yellow and black colors of its undersurface. Now it smeared itself all over with a musky substance from its cloaca. I reached down and touched it gently. It struck with mouth closed and thrashed about with renewed vigor—there seemed no end to its repertoire. I flipped it gently onto its back. It went rigid, opening its mouth and lolling its tongue to one side; its mouth became filled with dirt, lending credibility to its feigned death. This was the act of the famed "spreading adder." So stereotyped is this behavior pattern that it varies little from one individual to another. This one was almost a textbook case. If I turned it over onto its belly, it would instantly roll over onto its back again. (After all, any self respecting hognose snake knows this is the proper position to assume when you are dead.) The fact that these snakes put on such a convincing act is, ironically, often their undoing, as the violent display leads many people to believe that these harmless little snakes are deadly poisonous and so do not hesitate to kill them on the spot. Try as I might, I was unable to coax this little fellow into biting me—even when I stuck my finger into his open mouth!

In addition to the usual dune residents, there are occasional visitors such as the desert massasauga, or "pigmy rattlesnake," a small species easily distinguished from all other rattlesnakes of the area in having the top of the head covered by large scales called "shields" rather than by the smaller granular scales typical to the genus *Crotalus*. It was across these dunes that my nephews and I once tracked a juvenile massasauga for three hundred yards—quite a journey for a snake less than a foot long. When we finally caught up with him he was coiled beneath a small indigo bush. Had it not been for the tracks, he would have gone unnoticed.

Other not uncommon visitors include glossy snakes and long-nosed snakes, both harmless forms which feed primarily on the plentiful supply of local lizards, including the New Mexico whiptail—in which species there are no males—only females. They reproduce parthenogenetically. Scientists tell us that this occurs when gametes (egg cells) are formed from precursors that undergo an unusual type of meiosis in which a single, rather than double, cell division occurs. It may *sound* complicated, but this doesn't seem to trouble the lizard.

The dunes are also visited by an occasional badger or coyote, although I doubt that they are permanent residents there.

Perhaps the rarest resident of the region is the shy and inoffensive hook-nosed snake, whose most aggressive act is a sudden twisting of the body accompanied by a simultaneous eversion of the cloaca, producing a startling and surprisingly loud popping sound. To the unfamiliar this sudden display might prove sufficiently disquieting to allow the snake opportunity for escape. One night on the way home from the dunes I was fortunate enough to find an adult female, all of nine inches long, and obviously gravid.

I took the treasured specimen home and placed it among what I hoped would be comfortable surroundings in a five-gallon terrarium. The following morning I discovered she had laid three cylindrical white eggs. Not wishing to disturb the eggs, I immediately added water to the substrate until it appeared moist. I then covered the top with a single layer of Saran Wrap. This would prevent loss of moisture from the enclosure without suffocating the eggs.

I was concerned about the mother, who looked terribly emaciated. She refused all food (spiders, centipedes and small lizards) when offered, and I was saddened when a few days later I inspected the cage to find her lifeless form lying only a few inches from the clutch of eggs. The story has a happy ending, however, as all three eggs eventually hatched. The young were virtually indistinguishable from one another and were miniature replicas of the mother. They all twitched and popped enthusiastically whenever anyone entered the room. I carefully removed the young snakes and placed them in a clean muslin sack. Driving south towards the dunes, I located the exact spot where I had collected the mother. A lizard hole under a bush would be a suitable place for their release. After several photographs, I watched the young snakes disappeared, one by one, down the hole. [The dunes are now a subdivision. Box turtles and their brethren are being pushed closer and closer to the edge of extinction by development in central New Mexico.]

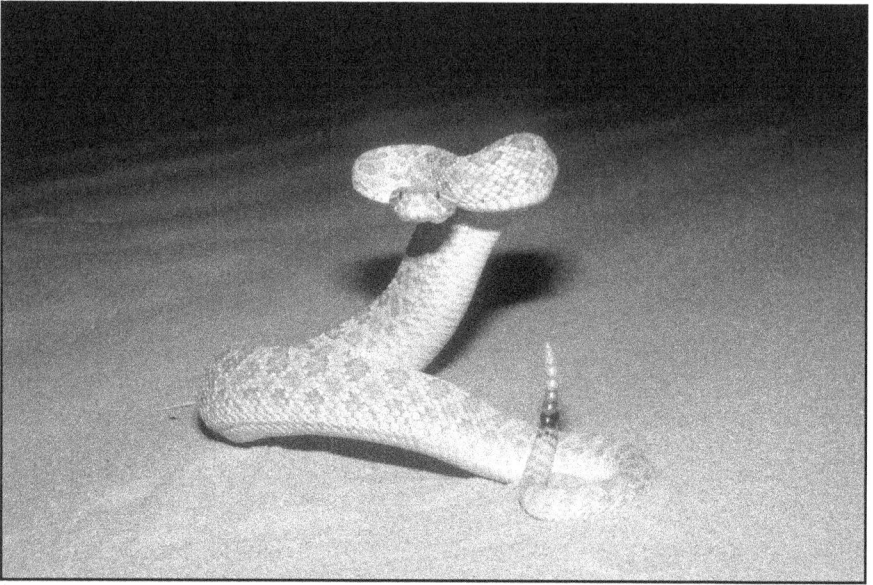

A prairie rattlesnake makes his stand at the dunes, Valencia Co., New Mexico.

Round-tailed horned lizard at the dunes. This lizard is smaller than a quarter.

Dark clouds roll in over the dunes as a summer thunderstorm approaches.

A hog-nose snake "plays possum" at the dunes, Valencia Co., New Mexico.

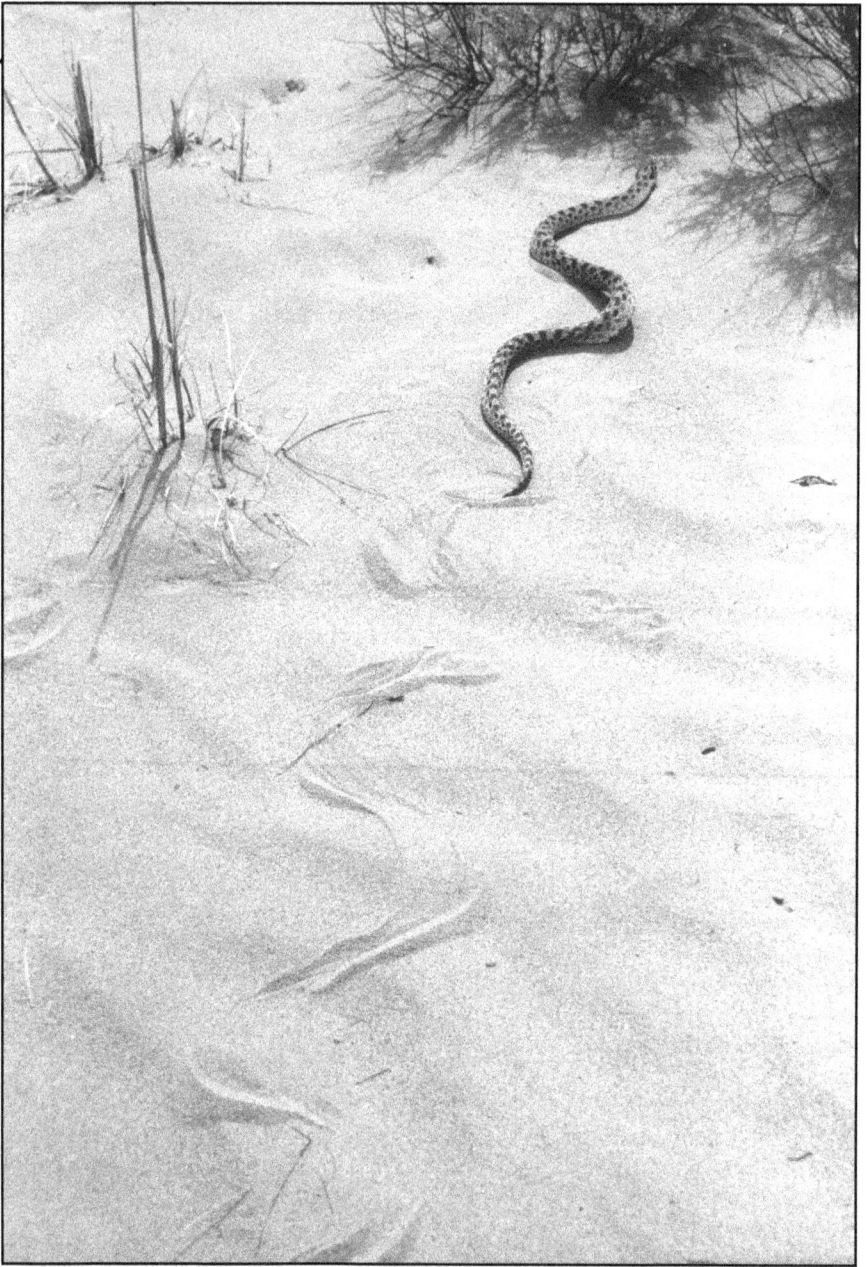

A hognose snake makes a well defined track in the sand at the dunes.

THIS PLACE IS A ZOO

In May of 1974 I joined the ranks of the Rio Grande Zoological Park in Albuquerque, New Mexico, and was immediately assigned to upgrade the reptile collection, if you could call it that. What little was left of it had been virtually ignored for years. I did what I could; cleaned out old shelters, mended cages, updated signs, set up an inventory system, and put together a group of volunteers who set about enthusiastically doing a variety of creative and helpful tasks.

In the fall of that same year the then director, Dr. Bruce stringer, (the second of five directors for whom I would have the pleasure to work) promoted me to the newly created position of Zoologist (later, Curator). I now dove headlong into my most ambitious project, the design and construction of a full fledged reptile facility, the centerpiece of which would be the Komodo Dragon Exhibit. I put together a training program so that I might have a professional staff to man the exhibit and was made a Professional Fellow of the American Association of Zoological Parks and Aquariums. An architect was hired to work with me and together we put in many long and arduous hours. We toured the country, talking to the "best and the brightest." People like Tommy Logan, Joseph Laszlo, J.P. Jones, John E. Werler, Howard Lawler, and Dr. Walter Auffenburg. I even hired an engineering firm to design a state of the art environmental chamber. The whole thing was computerized. (The prototype cost seven thousand dollars.) I acquired a supply of antivenin from various sources and arranged to have it kept at a local hospital in case it was ever needed. I also put myself on the list to receive the *Federal Register*.

The day John Roth appeared at the zoo I already knew who he was. I'd met him shortly after the ouster of Ivo Poglayen as zoo director. Dr. Poglayen was a professional who was always able to make time for us ordinary people. Since then the zoo had essentially been run by the "zoo advisory board." A group of important people who, traditionally, knew nothing about zoos. (The director's position had become basically a caricature.)

Bruce Stringer was a good veterinarian; very good. But he was no match for the City. For whatever reason, he had to go. The trap was sprung the very day he returned from his father's funeral.

Months later I found my environmental chamber dumped in a trash heap behind the administration building. Somehow I wasn't surprised.

The zoo was now in the market for a permanent director. They interviewed several promising applicants. But, according to the "search committee," (a.k.a. the zoo's advisory board) none were more qualified than John Moore.

Shortly after John Moore arrived, "highly recommended" we were told, from Audubon Park in Louisiana, two Saurus Crane chicks disappeared. So far as I knew these were the first of their kind bread outside the Indian sub-continent. John told me he had taken them home, "to care for them," and they died. He later told me that I had given him the worst case of ulcers he'd ever had in his life. After that we didn't talk much.

John was soon followed to Albuquerque by his long time friend and bird curator, Fay Steele. An affable fellow. Fay didn't hang around for long, though, and was soon off on assignment to Indonesia in search of the endangered and elusive Pink Pigeon. He'd told me how he had once run all the way from the Atlantic to the Pacific Ocean. Quite a feat (even in Panama). Fay had two passions; birds and running. He excelled at both!

The director of the Albuquerque Museum had generously (and fortuitously) offered to help out with a grant application to the National Endowment For the Arts. The mayor had given his blessing. This created quite a hullabaloo with "the board" who complained that I had bypassed them, which I had. They conveyed to me that they had found "irregularities" with my proposal and that I was "being investigated." I put in a call to an old family friend, who also just happened to be the senior partner in the largest and most prestigious law firm in New Mexico. I didn't hear any more about it. I later heard from the grant people themselves that the city had **declined** the grant on the grounds that "They couldn't find you."

Now it turns out that the donor of a reticulated python had complained about its accommodations. A keeper showed up to say that she'd been instructed by the zoo director to move it. She proceeded to place it in a trash can and seal it with duct tape. I was later told that she had left the snake under a heat lamp. She returned from lunch to find it broiled like a lobster.

Then there was that unfortunate situation with the African Dwarf Crocodile. It wasn't eating and I suggested that it be fed I.P. Instead of doing it himself, our esteemed veterinarian, one Bret Snyder, sent his assistant who proceeded to suck the crocodile's liver into a syringe and, "OOPS!" immediately re-inject it. Within minutes the hapless animal was dead! Mistakes happen.

As the reptile project neared completion I was told to select three people I wanted to staff the new facility. I chose Ted Brown, and two other individuals who had previous experience working with the collection. I was now satisfied that there would be qualified people running the program. Not so fast! Within the week I was told that there'd been some changes. I could hire only **one** person, and **not** Ted.

They had their reasons and I had mine. The reptile building was completed in Spring of '79, **just in time . . . I quit!**

I popped into Dr. Degenhardt's office one afternoon and announced that I planned to write a field guide for New Mexico. He approved. I also gave Bill a list of field notes for specimens that were still alive and hadn't yet found their way into the museum. Later on, I mentioned the field guide to John (Applegarth) who was by now living in Oregon working for the BLM. After that, every time I spoke to him, he would ask when I was going to write the field guide. Finally, after several years, I said O.K. He then inquired, more as a suggestion, whether it would also include amphibians. I said it could. He agreed to supply locality data, and eventually, at the last possible minute (John's motto could be summed up in one word, "Procrastinate, procrastinate, procrastinate."), also proof read the species accounts. I still have the hand corrected pages that he sent me. With Paul Hyder enthusiastically on board, it was "full speed ahead," so to speak.

SNAKEBITE; HOW TO PREVENT IT, WHAT TO DO ABOUT IT.

In a publication of this sort I think that a few words on the prevention and treatment of snakebite might prove useful; especially in light of ongoing confusion and controversy surrounding the subject.

Snakebite is not a major medical problem anywhere in the United States. In fact, more people every year are actually killed by lightening or bee stings. But occasionally someone is bitten; usually through carelessness, quite often due to deliberate provocation. Most often, snakebite can easily be avoided by following a few simple rules. First, never intentionally antagonize or attempt to handle a snake unless you know for sure that it is harmless. Second, don't put your hands or feet where you cannot see. Instead of stepping over a rock or log, step on top of it or, if possible, walk around. Rule number three, always wear protective clothing when you know you will be in snake country. High topped boot, long pants and heavy socks are the rule. During the hot summer months, rattlesnakes tend to be most active at night. Sleep up off the ground when camping out. (There is an old and unfounded superstition that a "hair rope" is protection against rattlesnakes; don't bet your life on it.)

But, what should you do in the unlikely event that you or a member of your party is bitten? First, if possible, make a positive identification of the snake. Otherwise, the offending reptile should be killed and transported to the hospital along with the patient. Then don't do any more than is necessary. First-aid measures are often responsible for more damage than the bite itself.

Reassure the patient. A certain amount of anxiety is only natural but the hysteria often associated with snakebite is counter-productive and is usually out of proportion to the seriousness of the situation. The victim should exercise no more than is absolutely necessary; never run. Also, alcohol, like running, tends to speed up circulation, enhancing absorption of venom into the system.

A constriction band, not a tourniquet, may be placed between the bite and the heart. Gum rubber tubing works best for this purpose but any strip of clothing will do. This should not be so tight as to shut off arterial circulation and must not be left on for prolonged periods (ten or fifteen minutes). All jewelry should be removed quickly and the constriction band, if used, must be maintained proximal to any observed swelling.

Professional medical attention should be sought immediately, even in cases where local symptoms do not seem severe. Not only can a doctor administer, and test for sensitivity to, antivenin, but he is best able to treat any other complications that may arise. "Cutting" by an inexperienced individual is ill-advised, although suction, if applied quickly, may be of some benefit. Again, the key is "moderation." Remember that a large individual of the poisonous persuasion may have fangs in excess of two cm. This places the venom pocket in close proximity to arteries, nerves and tendons. So for those who feel that they *must* cut remember the cardinal rule, UNDER NO CIRCUMSTANCES SHOULD INCISIONS EVER BE MADE CROSSWISE TO THE LIMB.

This might also be as good a place as any to mention that while ingested venom is eventually neutralized by digestive enzymes, mouth sores and bleeding gums can be problematic. Cause for pause.

For those individuals whose work or outdoor activities cause them frequent exposure to poisonous snakes, especially in remote areas, a doctor should be consulted on the use of antivenin. In the event of its use, instructions, which are provided with the kit, must be followed precisely. Great care must also be taken to insure that the victim is not allergic to the serum, prior to injection, or shock and death may follow. One quick way to test for sensitivity to antivenin is to place a few drops under the victim's eyelids and then observe the patient closely for several minutes for signs of a reaction. Under certain conditions decadron and epinephrine are sometimes administered simultaneously with antivenin. This may forestall or moderate an adverse reaction.

Atropine is reportedly of some value in reversing neurotoxic symptoms and, in the case of severe respiratory distress, its use is clearly indicated as a life saving measure. It should, if at all possible, be administered under the supervision of a qualified physician.

In all honesty , I am not enthusiastic about fasciotomy in the treatment of snakebite. In only a very few cases is the procedure actually called for, and fewer doctors still are adequately trained to perform it, especially outside of Texas where it was pioneered. Elevation of the affected limb (above the heart) can effectively reduce swelling and may mitigate the need for more extreme treatments.

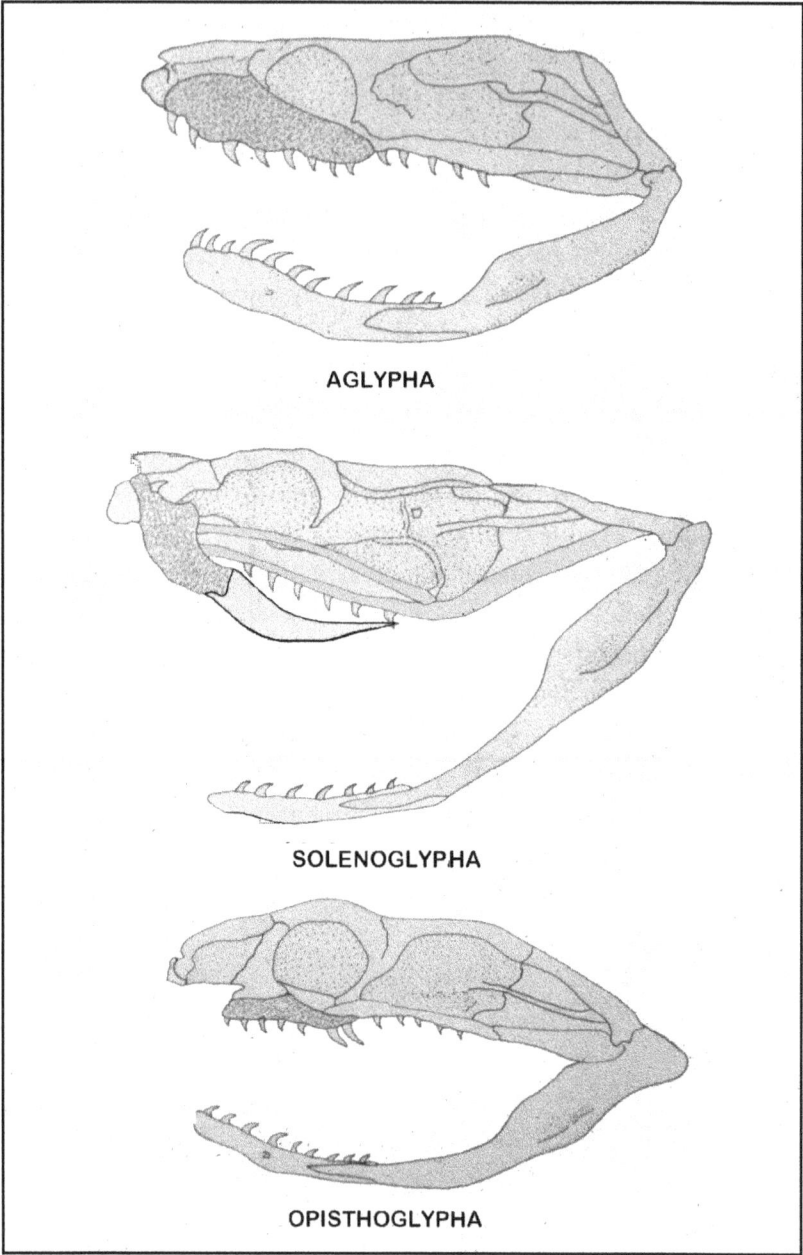

Fang types of various snakes; (TOP) non venomous [boas, racers etc.]
(CENTER) venomous [vipers and pit vipers including rattlesnakes]
(BOTTOM) rear-fanged [night snakes, lyre snakes and the African boomslang].

COMMON NAMES OF AMPHIBIANS AND REPTILES MENTIONED IN THE TEXT

(Common names are followed by equivalent scientific names.)

Alligator lizard (in Arizona), *Gerrhonotus kingi*
Alligator lizard (in Texas), *Gerrhonotus liocephalus*
Anaconda (snake), *Eunectes*
Animas ridge-nosed rattlesnake, *Crotalus willardi obscurus*
Archosaurian (dinosaurs and relatives), subclass *Archosauria*
Banded gecko, *Coleonyx variegatus*
Banded rock lizard, *Petrosaurus mearnsi*
Banded rock rattlesnake, *Crotalus lepidus klauberi*
Banded sand snake, *Chilomeniscus cinctus*
Black-headed snake (Baja California del Sur), *Tantilla planiceps*
Black-tailed rattlesnake (or black-tail), *Crotalus molossus*
Box turtle (western), *Terrapene ornata*
Bullfrog, *Rana catesbeiana*
Bullsnake, (or gopher snake), *Pituophis melanoleucus*
Bunch grass lizard, *Sceloporus scalaris*
California kingsnake, *Lampropeltis getulus californiae*
Camaleon (Mexico), *Phrynosoma*
Canyon treefrog, *Hyla arenicolor*
Chihuahuan ridge-nosed rattlesnake, *Crotalus willardi silus*

Chorus frog (western), *Pseudacris triseriata*
Chuckwalla, *Sauromalus obesus*
Clark's spiny lizard, Sceloporus clarki
Coachwhip (snake), *Masticophis flagellum*
Collared lizard, *Crotaphytus collaris*
Colorado River toad, *Bufo alvarius*
Common garter snake, *Thamnophis sirtalis*
Copperhead (snake), Agkistrodon contortrix
Desert iguana, *Dipsosaurus dorsalis*
Desert massasauga (or pigmy rattlesnake), *Sistrurus catenatus edwardsii*
Desert spiny lizard, *Sceloporus magister*
Diamondback rattlesnake (or diamondback), *Crotalus atrox*
Fence lizard, *Sceloporus undulatus*
Fringe-toed lizard, *Callisaurus notatus*
Garter snakes, *Thamnophis*
Geckos (lizards), family Gekkonidae
Gila monster (lizard), *Heloderma suspectum*
Glass snakes (lizards), *Ophisaurus*
Glossy snake (or glossy), *Arizona elegans*
Gopher snake (Baja California del Sur), *Pituophis m. vertebralis*
Gopher snake (or bullsnake), *Pituophis melanoleucus*
Gopher tortoise, *Gopherus agassizii*
Greater earless lizard, *Callisaurus texanus*
Green mamba (snake), *Dendroaspis viridis*
Green rat snake, *Elaphe triaspis*
Green rock (rattlesnake), *Crotalus lepidus klauberi*
Green toad, *Bufo debilis*
Ground snake, *Sonora semiannulata*
Hawksbill (turtle), *Eretmochelys imbricata*
Hognose snake (western). *Heterodon nasicus*
Hook-nosed snake, *Ficimia cana*
Horned lizard (or horned toad), *Phrynosoma*
Iguanas (lizards), family Iguanidae
Indian (or spectacled) cobra, *Naja naja*
Jemez Mountains salamander, *Plethodon neomexicanus*

King cobra, *Ophiophagus hannah*
Kingsnake, *Lampropeltis*
Leaf-nose snake, *Phyllorhynchus*
Leaf-toed gecko, *Phyllodactylus xanti*
Leopard lizard, Crotaphytus wislizenii
Lesser earless lizard, *Callisaurus maculatus*
Long-nosed snake, *Rhinocheilus lecontei*
Lyre snake, *Trimorphodon biscutatus*
Mamba (snake), *Dendroaspis*
Merriam's spiny lizard, *Sceloporus merriami*
Mexicna beaded lizard, *Heloderma horridum*
Mitchell's rattlesnake (or Mitchell's), *Crotalus mitchelli*
Mojave rattlesnake, *Crotalus scutulatus*
Monitors (lizards), *Varanus*
Mosasaurs (extinct lizards), family Mosasauridae
Mountain kingsnake (or mountain king), *Lampropeltis pyromelana*
Mountain skink (lizard), *Eumeces tetragrammus callicephalus*
New Mexico ridge-nosed rattlesnake, *Crotalus willardi obscurus*
New Mexico Whiptail (lizard), *Cnemidophorus neomexicanus*
Night lizard, *Xantusia vigilis*
Nile monitor, *Varanus niloticus*
Orange-throated whiptail (lizard), *Cnemidophorus hyperythrus*
Patchnose snake (Baja California del Sur), *Salvadora hexalepis*
Pigmy rattlesnake, *Sistrurus*
Pond slider (turtle), family Emydidae
Prairie kingsnake, *Lampropeltis calligaster*
Prairie rattlesnake, *Crotalus viridis*
Pterosaurs (extinct reptiles), order Pterosauria
Puff adder (snake), *Bitis arietans*
Rat snake (Baja California del Sur), *Elaphe rosaliae*
Rat snake (in Texas), *Elaphe subocularis*
Red diamond rattlesnake (or red diamond), *Crotalus ruber*
Red-spotted toad, *Bufo punctatus*
Reticulated python, *Python reticulatus*
Ridge-nosed rattlesnake (or ridge-nose), *Crotalus willardi*

Rock lizard, *Petrosaurus thalassinus*
Rock rattlesnake, *Crotalus lepidus*
Rosy boa (or rosy), *Lichanura trivirgata*
Rubber boa, *Charina bottae*
Russel's viper, *Vipera russelli*
Saddled leaf-nosed snake, *Phyllorhynchus browni*
Santa Rosalia rat snake, *Elaphe rosaliae*
Sheep frog, *Hypopachus*
Shovel-nosed snake (western), *Chionactus occipitalis*
Side-blotched lizard, *Uta stansburiana*
Sidewinder (rattlesnake), *Crotalus cerastes*
Skinks (lizards), *Eumeces*
Soft-shelled turtles, *Trionyx*
Sonora kingsnake, *Lampropeltis getulus splendida*
Sonora coral snake, *Micruroides euryxanthus*
Southeast Asia cobra, *Naja naja kaouththia*
Spadefoot toads, family Pelobatidae
Spectacled (or Indian) cobra, *Naja naja*
Spiny lizard, *Sceloporus*
Spotted night snake, *Hypsiglena torquata ochrorhyncha*
Spreading adder (or hognose snake), *Heterodon nasicus*
Striped whipsnake, *Masticophis taeniatus*
Texas horned toad (lizard), *Phrynosoma cornutum*
Therapsids (extinct reptiles), order Therapsida
Tic polonga (snake), *Vipera russelli*
Tiger rattlesnake, *Crotalus tigris*
Trans-pecos copperhead, *Agkistrodon contortrix pictigaster*
Trans-pecos rat snake, *Elaphe subocularis*
Tree lizard (in New Mexico), *Urosaurus ornatus*
Tree lizard (Baja California del Sur), *Urosaurus nigricaudus*
Turtle (painted), *Chrysemys picta*
Twin-spotted rattlesnake (or twin-spot), *Crotalus pricei*
Varanid (lizard), family Varanidae
Western diamondback rattlesnake, *Crotalus atrox*
Western whiptail lizard, *Cnemidophorus tigris*

Whipsnake, *Masticophis*
Whiptail lizard, *Cnemidophorus (Aspidoscelis)*
Willard's (or ridge-nosed) rattlesnake, *Crotalus willardi*
Yarrow's spiny lizard, *Sceloporus jarrovi*
Yuma kingsnake, *Lampropeltis getulus yumensis*
Zebra-tailed lizard, *Callisaurus draconoides*

INDEX

ABOUT THE AUTHOR

Michael A. Williamson was educated at the University of New Mexico. He is a former high school science teacher and was the first curator of birds and reptiles at the Rio Grande Zoological Park at Albuquerque, New Mexico. He is a former Professional Fellow Member of the AAZPA and a co-founder of the New Mexico Herpetological Society. He has authored numerous publications in the field of vertebrate zoology, including a guide to the reptiles and amphibians of New Mexico (also published by Sunstone Press). He has edited two newsletters and reviewed an article on gila monsters for National Geographic Magazine. He also served two terms as a delegate to the New Mexico Conservation Coordinating Council. He is married and has two daughters.

All life is defined by the inevitable unlikely event.
—Michael A. Williamson

www.ingramcontent.com/pod-product-compliance
Lightning Source LLC
Chambersburg PA
CBHW021332090426
42742CB00008B/570